P9-APK-178

THE HISTORY OF PRIVATELY CONTROLLED HIGHER EDUCATION IN THE REPUBLIC OF CHINA

The dissertation was conducted under the direction of Reverend Francis P. Cassidy, Ph.D., as major professor, and was approved by Right Reverend Joseph A. Gorham and Reverend Bernard T. Rattigan, Ph.D., as readers.

THE HISTORY OF PRIVATELY CONTROLLED HIGHER EDUCATION IN THE REPUBLIC OF CHINA

AN ABSTRACT OF A DISSERTATION

SUBMITTED TO THE FACULTY OF THE GRADUATE SCHOOL OF ARTS
AND SCIENCES OF THE CATHOLIC UNIVERSITY OF AMERICA
IN PARTIAL FULFILLMENT OF THE REQUIREMENTS
FOR THE DEGREE OF DOCTOR OF PHILOSOPHY

BY
ANTHONY C. LI, M.A.

GREENWOOD PRESS, PUBLISHERS
WESTPORT, CONNECTICUT

Library of Congress Cataloging in Publication Data

Li, Anthony C 1920-
The history of privately controlled higher education in the Republic of China.

Abstract of thesis--Catholic University of America.
Reprint of the ed. published by Catholic University of America Press, Washington.
Bibliography: p.
1. Universities and colleges--China--History.
I. Title.
LA1133.L48 1977 378.51 77-5797
ISBN 0-8371-9643-4

Originally published in 1954 by the Catholic University of America Press, Inc., Washington, D.C.

Reprinted with the permission of The Catholic University of America Press

Reprinted in 1977 by Greenwood Press, Inc.

Library of Congress catalog card number 77-5797

ISBN 0-8371-9643-4

Printed in the United States of America

Dedicated
in
Grateful Memory
to
The Late
Right Reverend Adam Paul Curran, O.P., P.G.
Prefect Apostolic, Kienow, Fukien, China

The History Of Privately Controlled Higher Education In The Republic Of China

Table of Contents of Dissertation

List Of Tables, Maps And Figures

List Of Tables, Maps And Figures (Continued)

Preface

The following pages contain an abstract of a doctoral dissertation: "The History Of Privately Controlled Higher Education In The Republic Of China." The Introduction, and Chapters III, V and VI are published in full. Only the summaries of Chapters I, II, and IV are published. Of the twenty-seven Tables, two Maps and two Figures, Tables I, II, III, IV, IX, X, XVI, XVII, XVIII, XIX, and XXVII, Maps I and II, and Figures I and II are published.

The general problem of this historical study was to trace the growth and development of privately controlled institutions of higher learning in China from the time of the Republic in 1912 to the present. Important phases of these schools - the history, student body, staff, organization and administration, curriculum, finance, buildings and equipment - have been treated. The study was undertaken with a view to showing the opportunities offered Chinese youth in privately controlled universities, colleges and professional schools for cultural, professional, and technological training before the Communists came to power. Specifically, the purpose of this study was to present a history of those private institutions that have been officially reorganized by the government, because only those schools registered with the Ministry of Education have legal status and definite standards.

No history of private higher education covering nondenominational, Protestant, and Catholic institutions in China has been written; nor has the present study claimed to be exhaustive. It is impossible to tell accurately the number of private schools of higher learning that have existed in China because reliable statistics are not available, especially for the earlier years. Many schools were incompletely organized and consequently, after a brief period of existance they closed, leaving no records. Some schools were founded by officials of the government and shared their prosperity or adversity. The classification of schools in the present study was based on information from the Second China Educational Yearbook issued by the Ministry of Education in 1948.

The history of private higher education in China may be conveniently divided into three periods: the Period of the Nationalist Government (1912-1936); the Sino-Japanese War and Postwar Period (1937-1948); and the Period of the Communist Regime (1949 to the present). Before the Republic, the system of education was based on the Chinese classics. It was an elaborate scheme of examination rather than of systematic instruction. Modern schools did not exist until 1905, when an imperial decree for educational reorganization was issued by the Manchu government, and the former program and method of examinations were abolished. With the advent of the Republic, a new system of education was inaugurated which extended from the kindergarten to the graduate school. In 1949, when the Communists came into power, a new era in the history of Chinese education began. Russian methods of education were introduced. Private denominational schools of higher learning have become government institutions.

The plan of the study was as follows: the Introduction treated of education in China and privately controlled institutions of higher learning before the founding of the Republic; Chapter I gave the history of nondenominational institutions of higher learning (1912-1936); Chapter II considered Protestant institutions of higher learning (1912-1936); Chapter III discussed Catholic institutions of higher learning (1912-1936); Chapter IV dealt with the further growth and development of privately controlled higher education (1937-1948); Chapter V presented the status of private higher education under Communist control (1949-1953); and Chapter VI was a summary of the results of the investigation.

The data were largely obtained from primary sources - annual government reports, bulletins, proceedings of national educational conferences, educational laws; the archives of the Benedictine Archabbey of St. Vincent, Latrobe, Pennsylvania, and of the Motherhouse of the Society of the Divine Word, Techny, Illinois. The Oriental departments of the libraries of Congress and Columbia University, Day Mission Library, New York City, the libraries of the United States Office of Education, of St. Vincent College, Latrobe, Pennsylvania, and of the Catholic University of America, the Institute of Chinese Culture, Washington, D.C., and the Holy Ghost Convent, Techny, Illinois, also furnished valuable source materials. Records, reports, catalogues, directories, newspapers, and annuals of schools were examined for pertinent information.

The writer is deeply grateful to the late Right Reverend Paul Curran, O.P., P.G., Prefect Apostolic of the Catholic Mission, Kienow, Fukien, China, and other American Dominican Fathers who sponsored his education and advised him on many occasions. He expresses his gratitude to Very Reverend Terence S. McDermott, O.P., S.T.Lr., Provincial of the Province of St. Joseph of the Dominican Order, and to Reverend Richard E. Vahey, O.P., Director of the Rosary

Foreign Mission Society, New York City, for the opportunity of pursuing graduate studies at the Catholic University of America. He acknowledges with deep appreciation the valuable assistance and kindly encouragement given him by Reverend Francis P. Cassidy, Ph.D., under whose direction the study was undertaken and completed. To Right Reverend Joseph A. Gorham and Reverend Bernard T. Rattigan, Ph.D., thanks are due for their critical reading of the manuscript.

He is sincerely grateful to Reverend George Putnam, M.M. who gave him counsel and advice in the pursuit of the investigation. His appreciation is likewise due to Reverend Mark Kent of the Maryknoll Fathers, Maryknoll, New York, Reverend William E. Fitzgibbon, S.V.D., of the National Office of the S.V.D. Catholic Universities, Chicago, Illinois, Reverend Sylvester Healy, O.S.B., Sacred Heart Academy, Lisle, Illinois, Miss Ruth Wilhelm, Associate Librarian, St. Vincent College Library, Latrobe, Pennsylvania, Mother Margaret Thoruton, former Dean of Aurora College for Women of Shanghai, Manhattanville College of the Sacred Heart, Purchase, New York, and Sister M. Mechtrend, S.Sp.S., Holy Ghost Convent, Techny, Illinois, for making available to him documentary sources.

Table I

Privately Controlled Institutions Of Higher Learning In The Republic of China

Date of Foundation	Institutions	Location	Control[1]	Type[2]	Faculty (1948)	Students (1948)
1864	Cheeloo University	Tsinan	Prot.	U	70	442
1870	Yenching University	Peiping	Prot.	U	267	901
1879	St. John's University	Shanghai	Prot.	U	165	1865
1888	Lingnan University	Canton	Prot.	U	104	1056
1889	University of Nanking	Nanking	Prot.	U	216	1084
1897	Hangchow Christian College	Hangchow	Prot.	C	72	889
1900	Soochow University	Soochow	Prot.	U	145	1626
1903	Aurora University	Shanghai	Cath.	U	145	1241
1904	Nankai University	Tientsin	ND	U	253	1066
1905	China College of Shanghai	Shanghai	ND	C	-	-
1905	Fuh Tan University	Shanghai	ND	U	334	3409
1906	University of Shanghai	Shanghai	Prot.	U	111	1064
1906	Peiping Union Medical College	Peiping	Prot.	C	43	69
1906	Nantung College	Nantung	ND	C	132	878
1907	Ming Hsien College	Chengtu	ND	C	43	247
1908	Hua Nan College For Women	Foochow	Prot.	C	55	222
1908	Kwanghua Medical College	Canton	ND	C	17	222
1909	Tsiaotsao Engineering College	Loyang	ND	C	27	174
1910	West China Union University	Chengtu	Prot.	U	255	1784

Table I-(Continued)

Privately Controlled Institutions Of Higher Learning In The Republic Of China

Date of Foundation	Institutions	Location	Control	Type	Faculty (1948)	Students (1948)
1910	Fukien College	Foochow	ND	C	74	948
1912	Tatung University	Shanghai	ND	U	105	2254
1912	Chunghua University	Wuchang	ND	U	106	1165
1912	China College of Peiping	Peiping	ND	C	139	3141
1912	Shanghai School of Fine Arts	Shanghai	ND	P	43	225
1913	Chaoyang College	Peiping	ND	C	83	1236
1914	Hsiang Ya Medical College	Changsha	Prot.	C	83	272
1915	Fukien Christian University	Foochow	Prot.	U	63	587
1915	Ginling College For Women	Nanking	Prot.	C	81	440
1917	Franco-Chinese University	Peiping	ND	U	92	495
1917	Min Kuo University	Hunan	ND	U	30	629
1918	Eastern Asia School of Physical Education	Shanghai	ND	P	31	133
1918	Tungteh Medical College	Shanghai	ND	C	51	491
1920	Wusih School of Chinese Classics	Wusih	ND	P	48	403
1920	Wuchang School of Fine Arts	Wuchang	ND	P	43	261
1920	Wen Hua Library School	Wuchang	Prot.	P	23	88
1920	Amoy University	Amoy	ND	U	176	1349

Table I-(Continued)

Privately Controlled Institutions Of Higher Learning In The Republic Of China

Date of Foundation	Institutions	Location	Control	Type	Faculty (1948)	Student (1948)
1922	Huapei College of Arts And Law	Peiping	ND	C	133	1075
1922	Soochow School of Fine Arts	Soochow	ND	P	40	194
1923	Tientsin College of Industry And Commerce	Tientsin	Cath.	C	91	761
1924	Shanghai College of Law And Political Science	Shanghai	ND	C	52	528
1924	Central China University	Wuchang	Prot.	U	58	537
1924	Tahsia (Great China) University	Shanghai	ND	U	136	2520
1925	Catholic (Fu Jen) University of Peiping	Peiping	Cath.	U	206	2383
1925	Kuo Min University	Canton	ND	U	-	-
1925	Southwest School of Fine Arts	Chungking	ND	P	34	92
1926	Tungnan Medical College	Shanghai	ND	C	56	416
1926	Kwanghua University	Shanghai	ND	U	155	1457
1926	Shanghai College of Law	Shanghai	ND	C	107	1103
1927	University of Canton	Canton	ND	U	173	2892
1928	Lisin Accounting School	Shanghai	ND	P	64	700
1928	Chengmin College of Arts	Shanghai	ND	C	48	219
1937	Northwest School of Pharmacy	Sian	ND	P	40	78

Table I-(Continued)

Privately Controlled Institutions Of Higher Learning In The Republic Of China

Date of Foundation	Institutions	Location	Control	Type	Faculty	Students
1938	Women's College of Catholic University of Peiping	Peiping	Cath.	C	-	-
1938	Aurora College For Women	Shanghai	Cath.	C	-	-
1938	Overseas Chinese College of Engineering And Commerce	Hongkong	ND	C	32	672
1938	China College of Textile Engineering	Shanghai	ND	C	44	74
1938	Han Hua College	Swatow	ND	C	28	520
1939	Ta Jen College of Commerce	Tientsin	ND	C	20	199
1940	Chiuching School of Commerce	Chungking	ND	P	54	123
1940	Chengfu School of Textile Engineering	Shanghai	ND	P	22	66
1940	College of Rural Reconstruction	Chungking	ND	C	43	264
1942	Chunghua College of Arts And Law	Canton	ND	C	-	-
1942	Shanghai School of Textile Industry	Shanghai	ND	P	46	346
1942	Southwest School of Commerce	Kweilin	ND	P	41	188
1943	Fuchen College of Law	Wanhsien	ND	C	30	801

Table I-(Continued)

Privately Controlled Institutions Of Higher Learning In The Republic Of China

Date of Foundation	Institutions	Location	Control	Type	Faculty	Students
1943	Chunghua School of Engineering And Commerce	Shanghai	ND	P	45	643
1943	Hsin Kiang School of Agriculture	Kiangsi	ND	P	21	157
1943	Nanfang School of Commerce	Canton	ND	P	71	687
1944	Han Hua School of Agriculture	Chungking	ND	P	27	66
1944	Chen Tseh School of Fine Arts	Tanyang	ND	P	37	104
1944	Chunghui School of Commerce	Nanking	ND	P	22	296
1945	Chih Shing School of Agriculture	Shensi	ND	P	26	162
1945	China School of Journalism	Shanghai	ND	P	35	686
1946	Chenyang College of Law	Szechwan	ND	C	35	783
1946	Chien Kuo College of Law And Commerce	Nanking	ND	C	48	493
1946	Chuanpei College of Agriculture	Szechwan	ND	C	58	462
1946	Hsiang Huei College of Arts And Law	Szechwan	ND	C	46	1092
1946	Hainan School of Agriculture	Hainan	ND	P	26	106
1946	Shanghai School of Dentistry	Shanghai	ND	P	24	68
1946	Northeast Chungcheng University	Mukden	ND	U	97	1409
1947	New China College of Law And Commerce	Shanghai	ND	C	132	878

Table I-(Continued)

Privately Controlled Institutions Of Higher Learning In The Republic Of China

Date of Foundation	Institutions	Location	Control	Type	Faculty (1948)	Students (1948)
1947	Kwanghsia School of Commerce	Shanghai	ND	P	24	128
1947	Kiangnan University	Wusih	ND	U	53	242
1948	Chuhai University	Canton	ND	U	44	565
1948	Chenghua University	Chungking	ND	U	-	-

[1] Control: ND-Nondenominational; Prot.-Protestant; Cath.-Catholic
[2] Type: U-University; C-College; P-Professional School

Introduction

A. Education in China before the Founding of the Republic

The history of Chinese education is almost the history of China. Perhaps in no other country has the educational process had such influence in shaping national life; nowhere in the world is learning more revered. Its ancient educational system is the oldest in history. It was democratic and static.[1] Educational institutions have a recorded history going back more than two thousand years before Christ. An elaborate educational system existed from the twelfth to the sixth centuries B.C. The Chinese classics became the basis of culture and of the social order. They furnished the substance of formal schooling.[2]

Prior to 1905, the government system of education was an elaborate scheme of examination rather than of instruction. Practically all schools were private. In the field of higher learning the government provided institutions known as Ta-hsueh in the towns; and as Kuo-tsze-chien in the capitals of the provinces; and the Hanlin or Imperial

---

[1]Patrick J. McCormick and Francis P. Cassidy, History of Education (Washington, D.C.: The Catholic Education Press, 1953), p.5.

[2]Paul Monroe, "A Report On Education in China," The Institute of International Education Bulletin, IV (Oct., 1922), 5.

Academy in Peking. They were mainly provided for the sons of nobility and the privileged classes. Education for the common people was largely left to local and private initiative. Schools were maintained by individuals, a clan, or philanthropic organizations. There existed also the semi-governmental institutions known as shu-yuan (colleges), which were founded sometime between the tenth and eleventh centuries. These colleges established by private enterprise were partly supported by the government.[3]

The purpose of training in ancient times was to develop talent and produce men of ability for the service of the state. The content of study was literary, and was dominated by the elements of Confucian morality. The Four Books and the Five Classics supplied the chief textbooks. From the days of the Chow dynasty they had formed the trivium and quardrivium of the Chinese scholar. The method of instruction was purely a training of the memory and consisted in the mastery of language forms.[4]

The examination system before the Republic was the only channel through which learned men attained positions of

---

[3]Monlin Chiang, "Higher Education in China," The Educational Journal, IX (November, 1936), 10.

[4]W. A. P. Martin, Hanlin Papers (London: Trubner & Co., 1880), p.123.

public service. However, it was very democratic. Any young men was eligible for the highest academic degree if he succeeded in the series of examinations. The people regarded him with deep respect, because they knew that he had earned his position by intellectural effort. The regular degrees were three: Siu-tsai or "Budding Talent"; Chu-lin or "Promoted Scholar"; Tsin-shi or "Fit for Office."[5]

The first of these is sometimes compared to the degree of B.A.; the second to M.A.; and the third to Ph.D. or LL.D. In addition, there was fourth degree known as Han-lin or "Forest of Pencils," which entitled the holder to be a member of the Imperial Academy. These degrees represented talent not knowledge; they were conferred by the state not the school; they carried with them the privileges of official rank. The best talent was admitted to membership in the Imperial Academy; the next best received lesser official posts in the capital or in the provinces; while the humblest spent their lives in teaching.[6]

Such a system not only led to the selection of public officials, but it also exercised a profound influence upon the mass of the people and the stability of the government.

---

[5] Ibid., p.64.
[6] Ibid., p.65.

There was no college or university in the modern sense, and no national system of common schools.

Toward the end of the nineteenth century, China was under the influence of Western countries and Japan. The Chinese Government had long realized that educational reform especially was necessary. In 1898, the young emperor, Kwang-hsu, issued decrees which called for the establishment of a system of modern schools, and a reform of the examination system. Unfortunately, however, the Boxer Movement which came to a climax in 1900 prevented these reforms from taking place.[7]

In 1901, Her Majesty, Tsu-hsi, issued an imperial edict establishing a new school system and abolishing the old examination system. The final collapse of the old literary order came in 1905, when a modern school system was adopted and the Ministry of Education was established.[8]

It is to be noted that the first more to introduce modern education into China began at the top, that is, it started with the organization of higher education. Many higher technical schools were established to meet direct needs

---

[7]Chai-hsuan Chung, "Tendencies Toward A Democratic System of Education in China," (Unpublished Ph.D. dissertation, Teachers College, Columbia University, New York City, 1922), p.22.

[8]Robert E. Lewis, "The Empress Dowager's System of Modern College for China," Review of Reviews, XXVI (July, 1902), 72.

in technology. The lower schools existed not for themselves but for the purpose of preparing students for these higher schools and the university.[9]

During 1902-1903 such institutions as ta-hsueh-tan (universities), koaten-shih-yeh hsueh-tan (higher industrial institutions), fa-chen hsueh-tan (law institutions) and yu-chi shih-fan hsueh-tan (teachers colleges) came into existence. The curriculum of these schools emphasized Chinese culture and encouraged studies in Western learning.[10]

According to the educational setup of 1905, the university was to contain: (1) a department of learned scholars; (2) the university proper; and (3) a preparatory school. The department of learned scholars was intended for research. The university proper contained the following departments: classics, law and government, literature, medicine, science, agriculture, technology and commerce. Both the university and preparatory school required three years each for graduation. There were also subdepartments, superior schools, and institutes.[11]

---

[9]Chi-pao Cheng, "Twenty-five Years of Modern Education in China," The Chinese Social and Political Science Review, XII (July, 1928), 453.

[10]Ministry of Information, China Handbook (New York: Macmillan Co., 1943), p.368.

[11]Chung-shu Kwei (ed.), The Chinese Yearbook, 1935-36 (Shanghai, China: Chinese Yearbook Publishing Co., 1936), p.460.

The school system of 1905 was greatly influenced by the Japanese educational system. This was particularly noticeable in the first Chinese plan of school reorganization and the curriculum of the university which were modelled after the Japanese pattern.[12] However, the policy of modern education was substantially the same as that of the old education. The same official degrees and titles were granted to graduates. The ultimate purpose of opening institutions of higher learning was the same as formerly, to train candidates for government service.[13]

Private schools of the old type continued. There was not a clear distinction between government and private schools. Many of the so-called government schools founded in and after 1905, were in reality schools supported by a government official, and shared his prosperity or adversity. Of the higher grade institutions, more than half of them were law and political science colleges. Many of these were private too.[14]

The educational reorganization of 1905 greatly stimulated the establishment of private schools of the modern type,

---

[12] Chiang, op. cit., p.10.
[13] Chuang, op. cit., p.23.
[14] China Educational Commission, The Report of the China Commission of 1921-22 (Shanghai, China: The Commercial Press, Ltd., 1922), p.27.

Table II

Privately Controlled Institutions of Higher Learning Established from 1864 to 1911

Year of Foundation	Name of School	Location	Type[1]	Control[2]
1864	Cheeloo University	Tsinan	U	Prot.
1870	Peking (Yenching) University	Peking	U	Prot.
1879	St. John's University	Shanghai	U	Prot.
1888	Lingnan University	Canton	U	Prot.
1889	University of Nanking	Nanking	U	Prot.
1897	Hangchow Christian College	Hangchow	C	Prot.
1900	Soochow University	Soochow	U	Prot.
1903	Aurora University	Shanghai	U	Cath.
1904	Nankai College	Tientsin	C	ND
1905	China College of Shanghai	Shanghai	C	ND
1905	Fuh Tan University	Shanghai	U	ND
1905	Yenching Women's College	Peking	C	Prot.
1906	University of Shanghai	Shanghai	U	Prot.
1906	Peking Union Medical College	Peking	C	Prot.
1906	Nantung College	Nantung	C	ND
1907	Minghsien (Oberlin-in China) College	Chengtu	C	ND
1908	Hua Nan College for Women	Foochow	C	Prot.
1908	Kwangtung Kwanghua Medical College	Canton	C	ND
1909	Tsiaotsao Engineering College	Loyang	C	ND
1910	West China Union University	Chengtu	U	Prot.
1910	Fukien College	Foochow	C	ND

[1]Type: U - University; C - College
[2]Control: ND - Nondenominational; Prot. - Protestant; Cath. - Catholic

and they were to be found in all parts of the country and were of various grades. The government's attitude toward these schools was more or less indifferent. It was laissez-faire, with minor exceptions, such as the prohibition of the use of real rifles in military drill, and the prohibition of the establishment of special schools for the study of political science and law.[15]

B. Privately Controlled Institutions of Higher Learning (1864-1911)

The first privately founded school by a Chinese individual was Nankai College of Tientsin, later known as Nankai University. In 1898, Mr. Yen Shiu, Vice-Minister of Education under the Manchu Government, invited Dr. Chang Po-ling to open a family school in his hometown in Tientsin. It was developed into a modern middle school in 1904 with 73 students. In 1906, it was moved to the southern part of the city, a section called Nankai, whence the name of the school. In 1918, it became a university.[16]

In the spring of 1905, students who had been studying in Japan were forced to return to China under orders from

---

[15]Hsin-cheng Shu, Source Book of the History of Modern Education in China (Shanghai, China: Chung-hua Book Co., 1929), II, 135.

[16]Catalogue of Nankai University, 1928-29 (Tientsin, China: Nankai University Press, 1928), p.14.

the Japanese Government.[17] China College of Shanghai was founded for them by some patriotic social leaders in order to permit them to continue their studies. Eight years later it was united to and became a part of the University of China in Peiping, which was established by a group of Kuomintang leaders. It was temporarily discontinued in 1917, but reopened a year later under the control of the Ministry of Education. It consisted of schools of arts, law, economics, and political science, and commerce. In 1932, it was closed by order of the Ministry of Education.[18]

Fuh Tan University was founded in the autumn of 1905 by students who withdrew from Aurora University.[19] Mr. Ma Shang-pei, an outstanding and well-known Catholic in China, was the first president. General Chu Fu, the governor of Kiangsu Province, offered his official residence for classrooms, and granted seventy acres of public land near kiangwan, Shanghai, for the erection of new buildings.[20] It gave four year courses in arts, science, law, and commerce.

---

[17]Shu, op. cit., p.262.

[18]Chi-pien Ting (ed.), China Educational Events of Recent Seventy Years (Shanghai, China: The Commercial Press, Ltd., 1936), p.267.

[19]Tang Yeh et al (eds.), Educational Encyclopedia (Shanghai, China: The Commercial Press, Ltd., 1933), p.1154.

[20]T. E. Hsiao, The History of Modern Education in China (Peking, China: Peking University Press, 1932), p.46.

From 1905 to 1911 it graduated four classes with fifty-seven graduates. During the revolution (1911), the school buildings were occupied by the army, and classes were temporarily suspended. However, in 1912, the school was re-opened, and in 1922 it was raised to the status of a university. Later it became a national university under the control and support of the Ministry of Education.[21]

The year 1906 saw the foundation of Nantung College. It was founded by the Chang Chien brothers as an agricultural school. A textile school, engineering school and school of medicine were established. Later in 1928, these schools were merged into a single institution called Nantung University.[22] Two years later the University was called Nantung College by order of the Ministry of Education. It had a textile factory, a well-equipped hospital, and over 16,000 acres of land for experimental purposes. It is the first modern agricultural school in China established by Chinese.[23]

During the Boxer Rebellion in 1900, some American Protestant Missioners and Chinese Christians were killed in Ta-ku, Shansi Province. In Memory of them a school called

---

[21] Ibid., p.47.

[22] Li-hua Chou, "The Nature and Achievements of Nantung College," Nantung College Monthly, II (July, 1947), 1-3.

[23] Ibid., 5.

Minghsin Hsueh-tang (Oberlin-in-China) was founded by Dr. H. H. Kung and American friends of Oberlin College, Ohio, in 1907. It was the origin of the present Minghsin College which was governed by Oberlin-Shansi Memorial Association, Oberlin, Ohio.[24]

In 1908, Messrs. Chen Tzse-kwong, Kuo Liang, and other interested persons established Kwangtung Kwanghua Medical Association to promote modern Medical training. In the spring of 1909, a college and hospital were founded at Tai-kong Road, Canton. In the same year it was officially approved by the governors of Kwangtung and Kwangsi provinces. Since then Kwangtung Kwanghua Medical College has become a centre of medical training for Chinese doctors and nurses in Southern China.[25]

Meanwhile the British Foo Company at Tsiaotsao in the province of Honan established a school of mining named Lu Kung College in 1909.[26] It was closed in 1912, but two years later it was reopened by the Foo Chung Joint Mining Corporation and named Foo Chung College of Mining.[27]

---

[24]Ministry of Education, The Second China Educational Yearbook (Shanghai, China: The Commercial Press, Ltd., 1948), p.738.

[25]W. Y. Chyne (ed.), Handbook of Cultural Institutions in China (Shanghai, China: Chinese National Committee on Intellectual Cooperation, 1936), p.142.

[26]Ibid., p.256.

[27]Ministry of Education, The Second China Educational Yearbook, p.742.

Since 1931 it has been known as Tsiaotsao College of Engineering.[28]

The last school established by the Chinese before the Republic was founded in 1910 by a group of Kuomintang leaders and called Fukien College of Law and Political Science. The present name, Fukien College, came into use after the College was reorganized in 1929.[29]

In the development of modern schools, China is greatly indebted to Christian missionaries. Long before Chang Chi-tung and others clamored for educational reform, the missionaries had pioneered in the attempt to make China acquainted with Western learning. In the sixteenth and seventeenth centuries (during the Ming dynasty) we find the Jesuit missionaries, Fathers Matteo Ricci, Adam Schall von Bell and Ferdinand Verbiest, having considerable prestige at the court in Peking because of their scientific attainments, especially in astronomy and mathematics. They were influential in introducing into China the knowledge of mapmaking, architecture, and mechanical devices.[30] The Catholic observatory at Zikaiwei, Shanghai, founded in 1899

---

[28] Ibid., p.743.
[29] Chyne, op. cit., p.95.
[30] F. L. Hawks Pott, "Christian Education in China," China Quarterly, I (March, 1936), 47.

by Father de Beaure Paire, is still an important center of scientific study. Here are published valuable bulletins which render service to navigators by forecasts of the weather, and of typhoons in particular. The Zikaiwei Library with over 200,000 volumes was founded by French Jesuits in 1847. In 1902, the Museum of Natural History, later connected with Aurora University, was started and became one of the finest of its kind in the East.[31] These are a few of the educational foundations established by Catholic missionaries in modern China. Apropos of them, Kenneth S. Latourette has paid great tribute to the genius of these early Jesuit educators, who "by their scholarship had enhanced the prestige of their faith and had aided in obtaining for all Catholic missionaries a hearing throughout the empire."[32]

The early educational work of the Catholic Church was confined largely to elementary education and consisted mainly of religious instruction. The only Catholic schools which were universally established were "prayer-schools," or catechetical schools, in which Christian children learned the catechism. The missionaries concentrated for the most

---

[31] "China." <u>Catholic Encyclopedia</u>, III, 669.
[32] Kenneth S. Latourette, <u>A History of Christian Missions in China</u> (New York: The Macmillan Co., 1929), p.175.

part on the apostolate among the Chinese masses. Although early missionary education was primarily designed for the children of resident Catholics, normal schools for the training of native catechists, and seminaries for the education of a native clergy were undertaken.

In the early years of the Republic, Catholic schools except in a few large centers, did not have the three levels: primary, secondary and higher. The scholarship of eminent Catholic missionary educators, however, and the high quality of their literary and scientific productions readily led to recognition of the schools with which they were connected.[33]

The term "college" used by Catholic educators was confusing because it was applied to high schools. According to educational standards of the government, many so-called Catholic colleges actually were senior high schools. For example, St. Ignatius' College and St. Francis Zavier's College in Shanghai, conducted by the Jesuit Fathers; St. Joseph's College in Hong Kong, conducted by the Christian Brothers; St. Paul's College in Szechwan; and other "Colleges" conducted by the Brothers of Mary, the Dominican Fathers, etc.; and a girls' college, St. John's College, in Hankow,

---

[33]China Educational Commission, "Christian Education in China," The Report of China Educational Commission of 1921-22 (Shanghai, China: The Commercial Press, Ltd.,1922), p.22.

conducted by the Canossian Sisters were in fact secondary schools.[34]

Catholic education eventually was to be found in every province and in every administrative district of China, including Tibet, Kokonor, and outer Mongolia. Non-Christian as well as Christian students were admitted to Catholic schools. The provinces of Hopei, Kiangsu, Hupeh, Shansi, Anhwei, and Szechwan had the largest number of students under Catholic instructors. Catholic higher education was strongest in cities such as Peiping, Shanghai, Tientsin, Hong Kong and Hankow.[35]

The following Table, derived from a study of the Annual of Catholic Missions in China, 1935, shows the status of Catholic education in China before the Second World War:

Table III

Catholic Schools in China (1935)

Type	Total No. of Schools	Student Body		
		Catholic	Non-Catholic	Total
Univ. & Col.	3	488	1551	2039
Secondary	102	5629	10890	16519
Higher Primary	447	11671	11994	13665
Primary	3430	71247	56286	127533
Catechetical	10464	122461	96031	218492
Grand Totals	14446	211496	176752	378248

---

[34]A Priest of Maryknoll, "Roman Catholic Agencies," Educational Yearbook, 1933 (New York: International Institute of Columbia University, 1933), p.572.

[35]China Educational Commission, op. cit., p.23.

Aurora University was the only university under Catholic auspices in 1903. The University opened in March of that year as a definite response to certain Chinese intellectual circles seeking a closer contact with European culture and science. Under the Chinese Chen Tan (meaning "aurora" or "dawn"), this University was founded by the French Jesuit Fathers at the suggestion of Mr. Ma Shang-pei, the "Grand Old Man" of Chinese literature. It beagn with twenty young natives following courses in French and philosophy. One year later the enrollment increased to one hundred and fifty students, almost all of whom were pagans.[36] Father Perrin and several associates were called in from the Anwei mission district to conduct the school. Barely two years in existence, the institution was forced to close when friction broke out between Mr. Ma Shang-pei and a clique of turbulent youth who demanded student control in the government of the school. The students left in a body in the spring of 1904, and the institution was discontinued for more than a year. In August, 1905, it was reopened.[37]

The program of studies from the beginning comprised courses

---

[36]F. A. Rouleau, "Chen Tan: A Chinese Catholic University," America, L (December, 1933), 295.

[37]China Synodal Commission, "Aurora University", Digest of the Synodal Commission, I (November, 1928), 414.

in French, English, European literature, the history and geography of China and of foreign countries, political economy, civil and international law, mathematics, and the natural sciences. It was the same as that leading to the French degrees of Licence ès Lettres and Licence ès Sciences.[38] It included four years of study, one year of study in the preparatory department, and three years in the University proper. The government of the school was in the hands of a chancellor, rector, and president, appointed by a board of trustees with the approval of the Superior of the Jesuit Fathers in the local Catholic Mission.[39]

In 1908, Father Li wen-yu was appointed rector and Father Perrin dean of studies. In the same year, the University was moved from Zikaiwei to Dubail Avenue, Shanghai. In 1910, by an act of benevolent tolerance, students of Aurora University were permitted to sit for the entrance examination at Peking University. This was quite an honor, because it indicated the appreciation of the government for the splendid work and high standards of the University in the field of literature and science.[40]

---

[38]Rouleau, op. cit., p.295.

[39]M. M. Chambers (ed.), Universities of the World Outside U.S.A.(Washington, D.C.: American Council on Education, 1950), p.263.

[40]Joseph de La Serviere, "The Work of the Catholic Church in China," The Chinese Recorder, XLIV (October, 1913), 625.

Protestant missionaries came to China at a much later period than Catholic missionaries. School education was regarded as an important branch of their missionary work. Robert Morrison, pioneer of the London Missionary Society, arrived at Canton in 1807, where he founded a school with funds saved from his salary.[41] He died in Canton on August 1, 1834 after having served for twenty-seven years as a missionary in China. A society for educational purposes, named after him was organized in 1835. The Society opened its first school for boys at Macao, a Portuguese colony, and enclave of Kwangtung Province, in 1839, and a school for girls at Ningpo, a year or two later.[42]

Protestant higher education was not begun until 1864. Twelve Protestant colleges and universities were founded between 1864 and 1911.[43] These schools enjoyed prestige and leadership in the development of the modern educational program of China. But most of these colleges were, in the beginning, colleges only in name. Their primary purpose was to raise up and train a literate native clergy.[44]

---

[41]Alice H. Gregg, China and Educational Autonomy (New York: Syracuse University Press, 1946), p.12.

[42]J. Leighton Stuart, "China," Educational Yearbook, 1933 (New York: International Institute of Columbia University, 1933), p.301.

[43]F. L. Hawks Pott, "Christian Education in China," China Quarterly, I (March, 1936), 50.

[44]Tyler Dennett, "The Missionary Schoolmaster," Asia, XVIII (March, 1918), 211.

The faculty was made up largely of missionaries. Numerous scholarships were offered, and students were sent by missionaries to their own schools. The student body for the most part was Christian. The majority of the graduates of the colleges were employed in the missions as teachers and evangelical ministers. The colleges generally were small, local institutions, and largely denominational. There was little competition with other institutions of **higher** learning. The emphasis was on service and the meeting of practical situations rather than upon academic standards.[45]

In this early period (and in general until the establishment of the Republic in 1911 and later) the administrative control of Protestant schools was in the hands of missionaries. The money came almost entirely from abroad, with the exception of student fees. The atmosphere of the schools was religious. Religious instruction and attendance at church were required as a matter of course. This requirement was later changed under the Republic.[46]

From 1807 to 1860 Protestant schools were confined to the coast, mostly the southern half of the coast. From 1861 to

---

[45]Earl H. Cressy, Christian Higher Education in China (Shanghai, China: China Christian Education Association, 1928), p.18.

[46]Stuart, op. cit., p.307.

1877 the eastern part of the country had schools more or less. From 1878 to 1890 the missionaries were pretty generally active, except in the provinces of Hunan, Kweichow, and Kwangsi. During 1891 to 1900 mission schools became quite numerous. From 1901 to 1910 the increase in schools was most marked in the middle part of the country. From 1911 to 1917 there was a movement towards concentration in populous centers which were fairly evenly distributed.[47]

The first Protestant college foundation in China was in 1864 at Tengchow, in Northern Shantung, due to the efforts of Dr. Calvin Mater, a pioneer Presbyterian missionary. In 1882, work of real college grade was undertaken. This college was transferred to Weihsien in 1904, where, directed by a union of American Presbyterians and English Baptists, it carried on a school of arts and sciences. Meanwhile a school of theology and a school of medicine were established at Tsinan. These three colleges were later merged to form Shantung Christian University, known in Chinese as Cheeloo University, the first instance of the union of international and interdenominational missionary bodies for the purpose

[47]Charles K. Edmunds, "Modern Education in China," Bureau of Education Bulletin, XXXIV (1919) 50.

of furthering Protestant higher educational work in China.[48]

While at Weihsien, the College exerted a marked influence. When China adopted its modern educational system, the graduates of the College supplied a large of the demand all over China for teachers trained in Western subjects.[49] The first records of the school available date from the year 1873, when there were ten students. As the result of the efforts of the Rev. H. W. Luce and others, funds were subsequently secured for the transfer of the two former schools to Tsinan, where in 1917 the whole University was assembled on a large and attractive campus comprising nearly eighty-five acres. The registration of the University in 1917 was 283 students.[50]

The purpose of the University was training for Chinese Christian leadership, especially for the ministerial, medical, teaching, and nursing professions.[51] It maintained a school of arts and sciences, school of theology, school of medicine, University hospital, and extension department.

---

[48] Associated Boards for Christian Colleges in China (ed.), The Story of the Christian Colleges in China (New York: Associated Boards for Christian Colleges in China, 1935), p.5.

[49] Educational Directory and Yearbook of China, 1920 (Shanghai, China: Edward Evans & Sons, Ltd., 1920), p.50.

[50] Chyne, op. cit., p.52.

[51] H. G. Woodhead (ed.), China Yearbook, 1924-25 (Tientsin, China: The Tientsin Press, Ltd., 1925), p.234.

The undergraduate work of the University was carried on mainly in Mandarin as the language of instruction. In the senior grades, however, much of the work was in English. Of the teaching staff, about one-half were foreigners. From the date of its founding, instruction in the physical sciences and mathematics was emphasized. The University was later joined by the Medical Department of the University of Nanking, the Union Medical College of Hanchow, and the North China Union Medical College for Women. This union led to the merging of six independent schools. By 1905, more than a dozen missionary societies of the United States, Canada, and Britain shared in the enterprise.[52]

In 1867, the North China Union College at Tungchow was founded by the American Presbyterians with seven students. Three years later, the Hui Wen or Peking University was opened by the Methodist Episcopal Board of Missions.[53] Bishop Charles H. Fowler came from America to hold conferences in 1888, and the influence of his visit stimulated the work of higher education in the chief Methodist centers. He inaugurated the plans which resulted in the organization of Peking University by uniting North China

---

[52] Ibid., p.235.

[53] J. Leighton Stuart, "Formal Opening of Yenching University, Peiping," Missionary Review of the World, LIII (February, 1930), 98.

College and Hui Wen University into one. It was then decided to seek a charter for the University from the State of New York. An act of incorporation was passed on June 25, 1890, which made provision for a board of trustees in New York and a local board of managers in China.[54]

After the establishment of Peking University, Yenching Women's College which had been started in 1905, and North China Theological Seminary were united with it. During the early years of its existence, the English name of the institution was Peking University, but from 1917 on the name, Yenching University was officially used.[55]

St. John's College was founded in 1879 by Bishop S. J. Schereschewsky of the American Episcopal Mission who combined for the purpose two boarding schools known as Baird Hall and Duane Hall.[56] Although it was known as a college, for many years the work for the most part was of high school grade. All instruction was given in Mandarin. In 1882, the teaching of English was introduced and from that time English was used as the medium of instruction for all branches

---

[54]Eddy Lucius Ford, The History of the Educational Work of the Methodist Episcopal Church in China (New York: Christian Herald Mission Press, 1938), p.157.

[55]Chyne, op. cit., p.276.

[56]Woodhead, op. cit., p.233.

of Western learning. In 1892, the college department was organized, and the first class consisted of six students. The president was Dr. F. L. Hawks Pott.[57]

At first a three year course of study was offered, but later it became a four year course, corresponding to the standard American college. The first senior class was graduated in 1895. It was incorporated in Washington, D. C. in 1906 as a university with schools of arts and sciences, medicine, and theology.[58] In the same year the medical school of St. Luke's Hospital of Shanghai was affiliated with St. John's.[59]

By 1911, the enrollment was 124 students. Mr. Jenner Hogg's estate known as "Unkaza" was purchased adding about 12 acres to the University holdings. The library which was started with some Chinese books collected by Bishop Schereschewsky and housed in 1894 in a large room set aside for the collection, was gradually increased by a further addition of books in the English language. The University grow steadily and became one of the outstanding and oldest universities in China.[60]

---

57 *Ibid.*, p.234.
58 Chyne, *op. cit.*, p.231.
59 E. M. Dodd, "Medical Education in China," *Educational Yearbook, 1933*, p.116.
60 Chyne, *op. cit.*, p.232.

Mukden Medical College, later known as Liaoning Medical College, was established by Dr. Dugald Christie and Mr. Arthur Jackson in 1882, who were members of the United Free Church of Scotland.[61] At first they opened a school of medical training at the Hsienking Hospital of Mukden. The College and hospital were united and were closely allied with the other two missions working in Manchuria. This medical school received strong support from the provincial government.

The faculty of the College consisted of British, Danish, and Chinese members. The curriculum was modelled after that of the Scottish universities. The College depended almost wholly, with the exception of student fees, on voluntary gifts, chiefly from Scotland. It offered a five year course of study, one year in preparatory studies, and four in college work. For a time it was known as Mukden Medical University, and was so registered by the Ministry of Education of the Peking Government.[62] It was one of the nine Protestant medical institutions designated and fostered by the Medical Missionary Association in China. In 1929, Mukden Province was named Liaoning Province. Accordingly, the College was

---

[61]Harold Balme, China and Modern Medicine (London: United Council for Missionary Education, 1921), p.126.

[62]Dodd, op. cit., p.112.

called Liaoning Medical College.[63]

In 1888, the Northern Methodist Mission established Hui Wen College at Nanking. Three years later Christian College was founded by the Foreign Christian Mission in the same city. Another school called I-chi College was founded by the Northern Presbyterian Mission in 1894. These three colleges were conducted independently until 1910 when they were united into a university called Nanking University.[64]

The origin of this University was determined at the annual meeting of Central China Mission in 1891, when it was agreed that there should be only one higher institution of learning "having the status of a university" within the bounds of the mission. A constitution was adopted which provided for the incorporation of a board of trustees and for a board of managers resident in China.[65]

The original campus of the school consisted of eight acres. On this site a building was erected in 1891, which provided for five classrooms, a large chapel, and a dormitory for thirty students. In 1906, the campus had grown to fifteen

---

63 Ministry of Education, The Second China Educational Yearbook, 1948, p.167.

64 Ministry of Education (ed.), Summary Review of the Institutions of Higher Learning in China (Shanghai, China: The Cheng-chung Book Co., 1942), p.115.

65 Ford, op. cit., p.161.

acres on which were located four modern buildings. The student body in 1909 in all departments totaled 353 and the average income from students was about CNC$43 per student. The first class was graduated in 1897, consisting of three graduated in liberal arts, two in theology, and two in medicine. Eighteen were graduated in liberal arts in 1906.[66]

Mr. John C. Ferguson was the president from 1889, and continued so until 1897, when he resigned to accept the position of president of Nan Yang College, a government institution in Shanghai. In 1909, a union of the Christian, Methodist, and Presbyterian missions was agreed upon. The University of Nanking resulted, and in April, 1911, it was granted a charter by the Regents of the University of the State of New York.[67]

The history of Canton Christian College, later known as Lingnan University, dates from 1884, when two farsighted members of the American Presbyterian Mission in Canton, Rev. B. C. Henry and Dr. A. P. Harper, proposed the establishment of a college of high standards to serve South China under Christian auspices. In 1885, Dr. Harper went

---

66 Ibid., p.163.

67 Ministry of Education, The Second China Educational Yearbook, 1948, p.162.

to the United States and raised the initial funds of approximately $100,000.[68] In 1899, a school was started on a wholly nondenominational basis which was moved to Macao during the Boxer disturbances and remained there four years. In the autumn of 1904, it was moved back to Canton into temporary buildings on the new site at Kang-lo,two and a half miles east of the center of Canton City.[69]

Meanwhile Canton Medical College for Women was founded in 1899 by Dr. Mary Fulton, a member of the American Presbyterian Mission. The name of the College was changed to Hackett Medical College in honour of Mr. E. K. Hackett of Fort Wayne, Indiana, whose gift of money had made the erection of a suitable college building possible. Later it was affiliated with Lingnan University.[70]

On the east coast, Hangchow Christian College was founded by the American Northern Presbyterian Board in 1897, the outgrowth of a boys boarding school established in Ningpo by the same mission in 1845. It was moved to Hangchow in 1867, and by 1897, it had attained the status of a college. Since 1910 the Southern Presbyterian Board has cooperated

---

68 Edmunds, _op. cit_., p.53.
69 _Ibid_., p.54.
70 Chyne, op. cit., p.106.

in furthering the work of this institution.[71] In 1911, the College was moved to the new site which it now occupies. It enjoyed the status of a university until 1931, when it reverted to the status of a college, and was known in Chinese as Chih Kiang College of Arts and Sciences.[72]

Soochow University, founded in 1900, by the Southern Methodist Episcopal Church, traces its origin to three sources. The first was Buffington Institute founded in 1871 at Soochow by Rev. Tso Tzse Zen.[73] In 1879, this institution was moved to the present university site under the management of Rev. A. P. Parker. While the Institute in Soochow was preparing to play a large role in higher education, Dr. Young J. Allen was planning a college in Shanghai. The work began in 1880, by consolidating a number of small schools, which a few years later developed into the Anglo-Chinese College.[74] In 1899, Buffington Institute was discontinued. A part of the student body, together with some of the staff, was transfered to the Anglo-Chinese College. The College continued with success until 1901 when it was

---

71Associated Boards for Christian Colleges in China, op. cit., p.7.

72Ministry of Education, The Second China Educational Yearbook, 1948, p.733.

73John W. Cline, "Soochow University," The Educational Review, XI (January, 1919), 75.

74Ibid., p.76.

closed and a considerable part of the student body and staff was transfered to Soochow University.[75]

Meanwhile, Rev. D. L. Anderson established Kung Hong School at Soochow in 1895, in response to the demand on the part of the best families of the city that their sons have an opportunity of studying the culture of the New World. It had considerable success until the Boxer trouble of 1900, when it was forced to discontinue.[76]

At the turn of the century the Southern Methodist Board decided to coordinate all its educational work in eastern China into one system of elementary and secondary schools leading to a single institution of collegiate grade. To complete this system Soochow University was established in 1900.[77] The University was formally opened in 1901 with six instructors and eleven students; and with literary, theological, and medical departments. Later it was decided to transfer the theological and medical departments to the union institution in Nanking, with the result that these departments were discontinued in Soochow.[78] The University

---

[75] Ibid., p.76.

[76] J. B. Powell, "Soochow University Elects Chinese President," China Weekly Review, LXII (September, 1927), 106.

[77] Cline, op. cit., p.77.

[78] Associated Boards for Christian Colleges in China, op. cit., p.126.

was controlled by a board of trustees, acting under a charter issued according to the laws of the State of Tennessee and responsible to the Board of Missions.[79] In 1905, Mr. Chas W. Rankin was transferred from Soochow to Shanghai to undertake the opening of a school of law which was the first of its kind for mission colleges in China.[80]

Shanghai College was founded in the year 1906 by the Northern and Southern Baptists of America. Two of the leaders in the founding of the school were the Rev. J. T. Proctor, the first president, and Dr. F. J. White, president from 1911 to 1928, both of whom were from the State of Missouri. In 1908, the conerstone of the first building, Yates Hall, was laid by a well-known American publisher and member of the Baptist Church, the Hon. E. W. Stephens of Columbia, Missouri. Two of the earliest buildings of the College were built by the Baptists of Missouri: Breaker Hall and Eleanor More Hall. A part of the campus known as Southworth Field was purchased with funds willed to the institution by Dr. Southworth also from Missouri.[81]

When the College first opened in 1908, there were only eight teachers, four freshmen college students, forty-five

---

79Cline, op. cit., p.77.
80Ibid., p.75.
81"Descration of Shanghai College by Japanese Army," China Weekly Review, LXXXV (June, 1938), 41.

preparatory students, and forty Bible students. In 1911, the English name was changed from "college" to "university" in agreement with Chinese educational regulations.[82] It was the only foreign institution in which Northern and Southern Baptists cooperated. For this reason it was often designated as the "Baptist foreign mission capital of the world."[83]

Dr. William Lockhart, pioneer medical missionary of the London Missionary Society, came to China in 1859. Two years later he went to Peking and there opened the first Western dispensary of medicine. The eventual outcome of his efforts was the Peking Union Medical College established in 1906; and in memory of this pioneer, the premedical college building was called "Lockhart Hall".[84]

Dr. Thomas Cochrane, a graduate of Glasgow University and a member of the London Missionary Society, was elected head of the institution. He succeeded in uniting the efforts of six religious bodies in the project, viz., American Presbyterian Mission, American Board Mission, Methodist Episcopal Mission, Anglican Mission, London Missionary Medical

---

82"Shanghai College Now a University," Missionary Review of the World, LIV (October, 1931), 786.

83Tan Yeh, op. cit., p.1395.

84B. E. Read, "The Peking Union Medical College," Missionary Review of the World, XLIV (December, 1921), 925.

Association, and London Mission, each of these missions contributing the services of one or more doctors to the staff.[85]

Union Medical College of Peking was opened on February 12, 1906, with an entering class of thirty-nine students. The aim of the institution was "to give medical education to any person applying with a good preparatory education and sound moral character." The school was built with money subscribed from various sources including the Empress Dowager of China. The first class was graduated in 1911; sixteen of the original thirty-nine to enter obtained diplomas; and with one exception all took up work in the mission hospital.[86] Six English and American Mission Boards cooperated in the development and maintenance of the College until July, 1915, when the China Medical Board of the Rockefeller Foundation[87] assumed full support of the school.[88]

---

[85] Tan Yeh, op. cit., p.261.

[86] Edmunds, op. cit., p.63.

[87] China Medical Board of the Rockefeller Foundation was the agency by which the Foundation accomplished its work in public health, medical education, and war relief in China. According to the report of the Rockefeller Foundation Review for 1918, the China Medical Board was carrying on the following programs: (1) Development of medical schools in Peking and Shanghai; (2) Assistance to unaffiliated medical schools; (3) Assistance to hospitals; and (4) Fellowships and scholarships. But the Union Medical College of Peking was the chief agency by which the China Medical Board sought to further its aims.

[88] Chyne, op. cit., p.223.

Prior to 1903, the members of the Methodist Episcopal Mission in Chengtu, Szechwan, were planning for union effort in higher education. The Rev. H. Olin Cady was the first in charge of Christian educational work in Chengtu. By December, 1903, he had developed a school of secondary grade with an enrollment of 184. In 1906, land was purchased and buildings were erected for the opening of Chengtu College.[89]

Three years later the first union educational institution was undertaken. The West China Union University minutes for the year 1909, described the plan as follows:

> At the October meeting of the union it was proposed to unite the three missions' schools of Chengtu, viz., those of the Canadian Methodist Mission, the Friends' Foreign Missionary Association, and the American Methodist Episcopal Mission, the said union to take place in February, 1909, on the new property purchased for the purpose of a union Christian University.[90]

In 1910, university teaching was begun in the two faculties of arts and sciences. The catalogue of 1911 records that there were eleven students. The school eventually became a federated union university and one of the most significant institutions of higher learning in China. Its charter was granted by the University of the State of

---

[89]Ford, op. cit., p.164.

[90]Shuan-tao-chang Tang, "West China Union University," West China Union University Bulletin, I (April, 1944),1.

New York. It was controlled by a board of governors, resident in England, the United States and Canada, and directed by its own senate and faculty.[91]

Plans for organizing a woman's college led to the appointment, October, 1904, of a committee of three by the Reference Committee of the Woman's Foreign Missionary Society of the Methodist Episcopal Church with instructions to investigate the feasibility of founding a woman's college in Foochow. A tentative board of directors was appointed with Bishop J. W. Bashford as president. Later a tentative constitution was adopted; and the site was chosen for the college.[92] Accordingly in 1908, the Hua Nan College for Women in Foochow, Fukien Province, was opened with Miss Lydia A. Trimble as the first president. It offered only preparatory courses until 1914, when the college level was opened with an enrollment of five students. The cornerstone of the first building was laid in 1911. Its department of education met with notable success.[93]

Meanwhile in Nanking, courses of study of college grade were given in Nancy Lawrence Memorial Girls' School. Likewise, in Peking, Miss Luela Miner was the president, in

---

[91] _Ibid._, p.2.
[92] Ford, _op. cit._, p.165.
[93] _Ibid._, p.166.

1904, of a developing higher institution of learning for women.[94]

The attitude of the government toward mission schools, Catholic and Protestant, previous to 1913 was one of indifference. The government felt that the regulation requiring that schools established by foreigners be registered was sufficient guarantee against any infringement upon the nation's rights in the field of education. The attitude of the government is seen in part from a statement issued by the Ministry of Instruction of the Manchu Government in 1906.

> Regarding schools established by foreigners in the interior, the Imperial School Regulations issued in 1903 do not apply to them. The fact that those that have already been established are allowed to function without being approved for the time being does not mean that if there should be any foreigners' petitions for the establishment of schools in the interior in the future that permission will be granted to open schools. None of the students already enrolled in private schools shall be given government rewards or encouragement.[95]

---

[94] *Ibid.*, p.167.

[95] Shu Hsin-cheng (ed.), "Correspondence to the Governors of the Provinces that permission will not be granted to foreigners to establish schools," *Historical Materials on Modern Chinese Education*, II, 135.

Table IV

Privately Controlled Institutions of Higher Learning in China (1912-48)

Year	Total No. of Institutions (Public & Private)	Private Institutions Total	Universities	Colleges	Prof. Sch.	Percentage of Private Schools
1912	115	36	2		34	31.3
1913	115	37	4		33	30.4
1914	102	28	4		24	27.4
1915	104	34	7		27	32.7
1916	86	28	7		21	32.5
1917	-	-	7		-	-
1918	89	28	7		21	31.4
1919	-	-	7		-	-
1920	87	25	8		17	28.8
1921	-	-	11		-	-
1922	-	-	11		-	-
1923	-	-	12		-	-
1924	-	-	12		-	-
1925	108	40	24		16	37.2
1926	-	-	30		-	-
1927	-	-	21		-	-
1928	74	26	21		5	35.1
1929	76	26	21		5	34.2
1930	86	33	27		6	38.3

Table IV - (Continued)

Year	Total No. of Institutions (Public & Private)	Private Institutions				Percentage of Private Schools
		Total	Universities	Colleges	Prof. Sch.	
1931	103	47	19	18	10	45.1
1932	103	46	19	19	8	44.1
1933	108	51	20	22	9	47.2
1934	110	51	20	22	9	46.3
1935	108	53	20	24	9	49.1
1936	108	53	20	22	11	49.1
1937	91	47	18	20	9	51.6
1938	97	47	18	20	9	49.5
1939	101	45	18	19	8	44.5
1940	113	51	18	21	12	45.1
1941	129	52	18	20	14	40.3
1942	132	51	18	19	14	38.6
1943	133	50	18	19	13	37.6
1944	145	54	18	20	16	30.3
1945	141	54	16	22	16	38.3
1946	185	64	22	24	18	34.6
1947	207	79	24	31	24	38.2
1948	207	79	24	31	24	38.2

Chapter I

Nondenominational Institutions of Higher Learning (1912-36)

From 1912 to 1936 there were thirty-one nondenominational institutions of higher learning in China, including eight founded before the Republic. Of these, eleven were universities, thirteen independent colleges, and seven professional schools. The number of institutions appearing in each of these catagories varied from year to year until 1929, when the Ministry of Education of the Nationalist Government adopted a new school system and issued the basic laws governing higher education.[1] They were established by philanthropic, social, and religious organizations, and private individuals. They were distributed throughout five main districts: North China, Central China, East China, South China, and Northwest China.[2]

In 1912, four new institutions of higher learning, namely, Tatung University of Shanghai, Chunghua University of Wuchang, China College of Peiping, and Shanghai School of

---

[1]Ministry of Education, "Laws On Universities," Laws and Ordinances On Education (Nanking, China: Ministry of Education, 1945), p.35.

[2]Ministry of Education, The Second China Educational Yearbook, 1948 (Shanghai, China: The Kai-ming Book Co., 1948), p.145.

Fine Arts were established by Chinese private enterprise. In the following year Chaoyang College of Peiping came into existence.[3] From 1917 to 1928, twenty-six institutions of higher learning were founded in seven provinces. The first privately controlled institution of higher learning registered in the Ministry of Education was Amoy University in 1920. Two institutions of higher learning, Nankai University and Chaoyang College, offered graduate work and conferred the Master of Arts degree. The others awarded only bachelor degrees in arts and sciences.[4]

The universities were divided into "colleges" based on certain subjects or groups of subjects, for example, the liberal arts, sciences, law, commerce, agriculture, medicine, and so on. These colleges were divided for purposes of organization and teaching into departments. There were universities with five, six or seven colleges; some had only three in order to be recognized by the state; and others had less than three. The university and college course lasted four years, except in the case of medicine which was six years and some professional schools, three years. It

---

[3]W. Y. Chyne (ed.), Handbook of Cultural Institutions in China (Shanghai, China: Chinese National Committee On Intellectual Cooperation, 1936), p.132.

[4]Ministry of Education, The Second China Educational Yearbook, 1948 , p.1406.

was common for the university and college to require students, after entering the school, to take a two year preparatory course, with much the same curriculum as the senior secondary school. This requirement was abolished, however, by order of the Ministry of Education in 1929 and since then, only graduates from senior middle schools have been permitted to enter the university.[5]

For the internal organization, each school was organized in accordance with the regulations and requirements of each category as laid down by the Ministry of Education. Generally speaking, they were similar in organization. Each school was governed by a board of trustees with a fixed number of members which had the power to establish the general policy, to manage the sources of finance, and to appoint the president of the school. Under the president were provided offices of studies, discipline, and business management, each with a certain number of divisions and a respective dean. In addition, there were special committees that dealt with entrance examinations, scholarship funds, library, publications, and building program; all of these varied from school to school.[6]

---

[5]Ministry of Education, Rivised Regulations for Private Schools (Nanking, China: Ministry of Education, 1933), p.3.

[6]Ministry of Education, Summary Review of the Institutions of Higher Learning in China (Shanghai, China: The Ching-chung Book Co., 1942), p.115.

The curriculum of the institution was outlined by the Ministry of Education with minor differences. The students attended classes for a little more than eight months. The academic year was from September 1st to the latter part of January, and from February tenth to the end of June. The number of extracurricular activities varied from school to school. Among them were student government, clubs, and athletic teams. They were under the guidance of professors and the general supervision of school authorities.[7] The sources of annual income likewise varied from institution to institution. However, most of them derived funds from student fees, private donations, invested funds, and government subsidies.[8]

Between 1926 and 1927, due to political unrest, some institutions, such as Chunghua University of Wuchang, Shanghai College of Law and Political Science, Shanghai School of Fine Arts, and Wuchang School of Fine Arts were temporarily discontinued; the others, however, continued to function but with declining enrollment.[9] After the Nationalist Government was established at Nanking in 1928,

---

[7]Ministry of Education, List of University Courses (Chungking, China: Ministry of Education, 1940), p.65.

[8]Ministry of Education, Summary Review of the Institutions of Higher Learning in China, p.121.

[9]Ministry of Education, A Collection of Important Documents of Education (Nanking, China: Ministry of Education, 1942), p.108.

it changed its attitude toward private schools from one of indifference to one of strict control. Each school was required to register and fulfill certain requirements in order to be recognized by the Ministry of Education. Many nondenominational institutions of higher learning obtained annually financial aid from the central government as well as from provincial governments. It is true, that as a result of government regulations some privately controlled institutions of higher learning consolidated or were reduced in scope, but these as well as public schools became more efficient and effective in their instruction, and enjoyed a brighter future.[10]

---

[10]China Yearbook Committee, China Yearbook, 1930 (Tientsin, China: The Tientsin Press, Ltd., 1931), p.530.

Table IX

Locations of Nondenominational Institutions of Higher Learning Before the Sino-Japanese War

Institutions	Cities	Provinces	Regions
Nankai University	Tientsin	Hopei	North China
Fuh Tan University	Shanghai	Kiangsu	East China
Nantung College	Nantung	Kiangsu	East China
Minghsin College	Chengtu	Szechwan	Central China
Kwanghua Medical College	Canton	Kwangtung	South China
Tsiaotsao Engineering College	Loyang	Honan	Central China
Fukien College	Foochow	Fukien	South China
Tatung University	Shanghai	Kiangsu	East China
Wuchang Chunghua University	Wuchang	Hupeh	Central China
China College	Peiping	Hopei	North China
Shanghai School of Fine Arts	Shanghai	Kiangsu	East China
Chaoyang College	Peiping	Hopei	North China
Franco-Chinese University	Peiping	Hopei	North China
Min Kuo University	Ningsian	Hunan	South-East China
Eastern Asia School of Physical Education	Shanghai	Kiangsu	East China
Tungteh Medical College	Shanghai	Kiangsu	East China
Wusih School of Chinese Classics	Wusih	Kiangsu	East China

Table IX - (Continued)

Locations of Nondenominational Institutions of Higher Learning Before the Sino-Japanese War

Institutions	Cities	Provinces	Regions
Wuchang School of Fine Arts	Wuchang	Hupeh	Central China
Amoy University	Amoy	Fukien	South China
North China College of Arts And Law	Peiping	Hopei	North China
Soochow School of Fine Arts	Soochow	Kiangsu	East China
Shanghai College of Law And Political Science	Shanghai	Kiangsu	East China
Tahsia University	Shanghai	Kiangsu	East China
Kuo Min University	Canton	Kwangtung	South China
Southwest School of Fine Arts	Chungking	Szechwan	Central China
Tungteh Medical College	Shanghai	Kiangsu	East China
Kwanghua University	Shanghai	Kiangsu	East China
Shanghai College of Law	Shanghai	Kiangsu	East China
University of Canton	Canton	Kwangtung	South China
Lisin Accounting School	Shanghai	Kiangsu	East China
Chengmin College of Arts	Shanghai	Kiangsu	East China

Map I: Locations Of Nondenominational Institutions Of Higher Learning Before The Outbreak Of The Sino-Japanese War

Chapter II

Protestant Institutions of Higher Learning (1912-1936)

According to the statistical report of the Ministry of Education in 1937, there were sixteen Protestant institutions of higher learning, including ten founded before the Republic. Of these, ten were universities, five were colleges, and one was professional school. The Protestant institutions numbered less than one-fourth of the total higher institutions in China. They were supported by thirty-eight different missions from America, England, and Canada. All were coeducational except Ginling and Hua Nan, which were colleges exclusively for women. In 1936, they were attended by 5,771 students, ranging from 16 in Wen Hua Library School to 772 in Yenching University. There were 1,054 teachers, and 412 officials. Eight of the schools were union institutions, maintained by several denominational boards cooperatively; while four were denominational. Two institutions, Lignan University and Hsiang Ya Medical College, were strictly nonsectarian, though they were begun and partly supported by Protestant missions.[1]

---

[1]Ministry of Education, The Second China Educational Yearbook, 1948, p.485.

NORTH CHINA: Cheeloo University combined five institutions into one and enlisted the support of twelve missions. Its medical school supplied large groups of doctors for the needs of China. The program of rural reconstruction, the use of Mandarin as the medium of instruction, and the strong emphasis on sciences and mathematics were its characteristic features.[2] Yenching University combined four institutions and was organized according to the central federated type in the Peiping area. It had the largest enrollment among the Protestant institutions of higher learning.[3] Peiping Union Medical College was the outgrowth of the Union Medical School founded in 1906 by six American and English Missionary Boards. From 1914, it was under the support of the China Medical Board of the Rockefeller Foundation. Its hospital was well-equipped with every modern medical device and was ranked the first of its kind in China.[4]

EAST CHINA: University of Nanking, founded in 1910, by the union of three separate schools, made exceptionally important contributions in the field of agriculture. It also had a strong department of sociology which did splendid

---

[2]China Christian Association, Handbook of Christian Colleges and Universities in China (Shanghai, China: China Christian Association, 1926), p.15.

[3]Catalogue of Yenching University, 1942-43. pp.5-8.

[4]Thomas Chu, Chinese Medical Directory (Shanghai, China: Chinese Medical Association, 1939), p.133.

relief work during the famine.[5] St. John's University, founded in 1879, by the American Episcopal Mission in Shanghai, probably had more famous alumni than any other institution, and had a first rate medical school.[6] Soochow University, an union of three distinct schools of Soochow in 1900, was the crowning institution of the Southern Methodist Episcopal Board in that area. It had a renowned law school and an outstanding department of biology.[7] The University of Shanghai, established in 1916, by the Northern and Southern Baptists of America, had a good school of Commerce.[8] Hangchow Christian College, founded in 1879, as a denominational institution, was supported by the North Presbyterian Board of the United States and had a promising school of engineering.[9]

SOUTH CHINA: Although Lingnan University was regarded

5University of Nanking, "List of Educational Events of the University of Nanking," Nanking University Bulletin, CCCXL (June, 1944), 2.

6Publication Committee of St. John's University, St. John's University, 1879-1929 (Shanghai, China: Kelly and Walsh, Ltd., 1929), pp.24-25.

7Soochow University, Twenty-fifth Anniversary of Soochow University (Soochow, China: Soochow University Press, 1925), p.7.

8Catalogue of the University of Shanghai, 1936-37, p.3.

9Associated Boards for Christian Colleges in China, The Story of the Christian Colleges in China (New York: Associated Boards for Christian Colleges in China, 1935), p.6.

Table X

Protestant Institutions of Higher Learning (1864-1924)

Date Founded	Name	Place Incorporated	No. of Mission Boards	Year Registered	Location
1864	Cheeloo University	Canada	12	1931	Tsinan
1870	Yenching University	New York	4	1929	Peiping
1879	St. John's University	D.C.	1	1947	Shanghai
1888	Lingnan University	New York	0	1930	Canton
1889	Nanking University	New York	5	1928	Nanking
1897	Hangchow Christian Col.	D.C.	2	1931	Hangchow
1900	Soochow University	Tennessee	1	1929	Soochow
1906	University of Shanghai	Virginia	3	1929	Shanghai
1906	Peiping Union Medical College	New York	6	1930	Peiping
1908	Hua Nan College for Women	New York	1	1933	Foochow
1910	West China Union Univ.	New York	8	1933	Chengtu
1914	Hsiang Ya Medical Col.	Connecticut	1	1931	Changsha
1915	Fukien Christian Univ.	New York	5	1931	Foochow
1915	Ginling College for Women	New York	8	1930	Nanking
1920	Wen Hua Library School	New York	2	1929	Wuchang
1924	Central China University	New York	5	1931	Wuchang
Totals	16		64		

as nonsectarian, and had a strong Chinese constituency in the Kwangtung area, its faculty was composed of teachers of fifteen denominations from America and England. It carried on many scientific experiments in agriculture, and made important contributions to the culture of South China.[10] Fukien Union University was inaugurated in 1911, by six missions working in Fukien Province. It had a highly developed premedical school situated on a beautiful site comprising both plain and hilltop.[11]

CENTRAL CHINA: Central China University combined three colleges in Wuchang and Hankow in 1924, and was supported by five missionary societies in those areas. Its laboratories were well-equipped, and the school was considered the center of science in Central China.[12] Hsiang Ya Medical College was established in 1914, by joint efforts of the Yale Foreign Missionary Society and the Yu-chuan Educational Association. It had the support of Yale University students and alumni. Its hospital ranked second only

---

[10] Lingnan University Bulletin, VI (October, 1933),28-41.

[11] Edwin C. Jones, "Fukien Christian University," The China Mission Yearbook, 1918, E.C. Lobenstine and A. L. Warnshuis, editors (Shanghai, China: Kwang Hsueh Publishing House, 1918), p.187.

[12] Ministry of Education, The Report On the Education of the Provinces of Hupeh and Kiangsi (Nanking, China: Ministry of Education, 1933), p.92

to the Hospital of Peiping Union Medical College.[13] Wuchang Wen Hua Library School was founded by Miss Elizabeth Wood in 1910, as a department of Boone University and became an independent school in 1929. The school trained librarians and led to the development of the public library movement in China.[14]

WOMEN'S COLLEGES: Protestant missionaries are also to be credited as the pioneers in the establishment of colleges for women in China. Hua Nan College for Women, founded in 1908, by the Foreign Missionary Society of the Methodist Episcopal Church of the United States, was the first college for women in Southern China. It had a strong department of education, and the majority of its graduates became teachers.[15] Ginling College for Women, established in 1915, by three missions in the Nanking area, not only trained physical education teachers and social workers, but also provided wholesome wives and mothers.[16]

The Protestant institutions of higher learning were established with a two-fold purpose: first, to assist in

---

13Ministry of Education, The Second China Educational Yearbook, 1948, p.691.

14Samuel T. Y. Seng, "Miss Mary Elizabeth Wood, the Queen of the Modern Library Movement in China," Boone Library School Quarterly, III (September, 1931), 8-11.

15Catalogue of the Hua Nan College for Women. 1934-35, p.3.

16Eddy L. Ford, The History of the Educational Work of the Methodist Episcopal Church in China (New York: Christian Herald Mission Press, 1938), p.255.

providing higher education for the youth of China; second, to assist directly or indirectly in the propagation of the Protestant Christian religion.[17] The financial support of these institutions came partly from the United Boards of America, England, and Canada, and partly from the alumni, student fees, government grants, school funds, and private gifts. The China Medical Board of the Rockefeller Foundation generously assisted certain medical schools, and supplied equipment for the laboratories of the Protestant colleges.[18]

The buildings of the Protestant institutions of higher learning for the most part were good. Many of the newer buildings were an adaptation of the Chinese style of architecture.[19] The curricula conformed with the standards set by the West. Religion was taught both during and outside school hours. Government regulations permitted it as an elective.[20]

In the beginning, the Chinese government neither recognized

---

[17]Leighton Stuart, "China," Educational Yearbook,1933 (New York: International Institute, Teachers College, Columbia University, 1933), p.319.

[18]Earl H. Cressy, Christian Higher Education in China (Shanghai, China: China Christian Educational Association, 1928), pp.17-38.

[19]*Ibid*., p.45.

[20]Earl H. Cressy, "Correlated Program for Christian Higher Education in China," International Review of Missions, XXII (April, 1933), 240-41.

nor granted charters to mission schools. In order to gain recognition, Protestant institutions of higher learning had to obtain charters from the states of New York, Tennessee, Virginia, Connecticut; and from Washington, D.C., and Ontario, Canada.[21] After formulating a system of modern education and laying down regulations for private schools in 1928, the Chinese government required mission schools to conform to the national plan. All Protestant institutions of higher learning were registered with the Ministry of Education. The president and a majority of the members of the board of directors were Chinese. However, Chinese leadership did not tend to lessen the Christian character of the schools. The board of directors made little real difference as to church control, for the members of the board were generally Protestant.[22]

The Protestant institutions of higher learning appeared to enjoy a gratifying measure of public confidence. They labored successfully in the formation of character through

---

[21]Ministry of Education, A Collection of Important Educational Laws and Regulations (Nanking, China: Ministry of Education, 1930), p.46.

[22]W. T. Tao and C. P. Chen, Education in China (Shanghai, China: The Commercial Press, Ltd., 1925), p.37.

religious instruction, and the influence of missionaries. Compared to the government institutions, there was more stability, and more effective intellectual discipline both in the student body and in the faculty.[23]

---

[23]*Ibid.*, p.39.

Table XVI

Protestant Missions Cooperating With Private Institutions of Higher Learning

Year of Entrance	Protestant Missions
1830	American Board of Commissioners for Foreign Missions
1834	American Baptist Foreign Missionary Society
1835	American Protestant Episcopal Board
1838	American Presbyterian Mission, North
1842	Board of Foreign Missions of Reformed Church in America
1845	British Church Missionary Society
1847	Board of Foreign Missions of the Methodist Episcopal Church, North
1847	Board of Foreign Missions of the Seven Days Baptist Church
1847	Board of Foreign Missions of the Southern Baptist Convention
1847	English Presbyterians
1847	Basel Missionary Society
1847	Rhenish Missionary Society
1848	Board of Foreign Missions of the Methodist Episcopal Church, South
1852	Wesleyan Missionary Society
1860	English Methodist New Connection
1864	American Presbyterian Mission, South
1864	English Methodist Free Church
1865	China Island Mission
1869	Women's Union Missionary Society of America

Table XVI - (Continued)

Protestant Missions Cooperating With Private Institutions of Higher Learning

Year of Entrance	Protestant Missions
1871	Presbyterian Church, Canada
1876	American Bible Society
1882	Berlin Missionary Society
1886	Foreign Christian Missionary Society
1887	China Blind Mission
1888	United Christian Missionary Society
1889	United Brethren in Christ
1890	Swedist-American Mission
1891	American Friends' Foreign Mission Association
1891	Methodist Episcopal Church, Canada
1892	Gospel Baptist Mission
1895	Y. M. C. A. in Foreign Lands Society
1896	Reformed Presbyterians
1897	Comberland Presbyterians

Data from _Statistics of Protestant Missions in China_. New York: United Board of Christian Colleges in China, 1935. P.16.

Chapter III

Catholic Institutions of Higher Learning (1912-36)

The purpose of Catholic missions in China was primarily apostolic work among the people. The priests with the aid of Sisters labored to form parishes since they are basic to the establishment of a native church. Catholic missionaries lived very close to the life of the common people. They endured privations, suffered hardships, yet remained faithful to the charge entrusted to them. They had wide learning and supplemented it with a mastery of Chinese in its spoken and written forms. Consequently they received deep respect from the Chinese people.

Though Catholic missionaries came to China in the sixteen century, their educational work was of necessity confined to the elementary level and consisted largely of religious instruction. Education on Western lines was organized by them in 1852, when a college for the education of native priests was opened.[1] It was not until the early years of the twentieth century that they founded schools of higher learning in which a general education

---

[1]McCormich and Cassidy, History of Education, p.15.

was given.

Catholic educators were aware of the need of educating Chinese Catholic youth in such a way as to make them competent to serve in public life and to share in the modernization of their country. For this purpose Pius XI, in an address to missionaries, urged the founding of Catholic institutions of higher learning.

> Do not content yourself with the building of hospitals and dispensaries and primary schools - institutions which are required everywhere. It is moreover very useful that you establish higher schools for young men, agricultural schools and industrial schools.
>
> It is also an occasion to exhort you not to neglect the leading and influential persons of the country and their children. It is true that Our Lord said Himself: 'The Spirit of the Lord had given me the mission to evangelize the poor.' But we must not forget the words of Saint Paul: 'I owe myself to the learned as much as to the ignorant'; and practice and experience teach us that the elite having once been gained to us in a country, the ordinary people follow easily.'[2]

The importance of establishing colleges in Chinese cities was stressed.

> It is a thing of the greatest importance for the Church and one which might have the greatest and widest influence in the great Chinese country. There is no one who denies that education today is the most appropriate means of apostolate in the conversion of souls in China. It has a lasting influence. The former Apostolic Delegate,

---

[2] Leo-Paul Bourassa, "Some Notes On the Apostolate Through Schools and Colleges," China Missionary Bulletin, III (May, 1951), 398.

> His Eminence Archbishop Constantini, affirmed this often and did not even hesitate to say that colleges in the main cities were so important that, if need be, rural missions had to be considered less important in order to organize colleges.[3]

According to the report of the Annual of Catholic Missions in China in 1935, the educational work of the Catholic Church up to that time had extended over the whole country and included every level, from the elementary to the university. The total number of schools which the Church maintained throughout China was 14,446. They were so widely distributed that in no province of China were there less than fifty Catholic schools.

The total number of students was 378,248. However, in the field of higher education, there were only three institutions. Of these, two, Aurora University of Shanghai and the Catholic University of Peiping, were fully accredited ta-hsueh (universities) with three colleges; while Tientsin College of Industry and Commerce (Hautes Études) was a hsueh-yuan (college) with two faculties. In addition, a hostel, known as Ricci Hall, which was erected in 1929, by the Fathers of the Society of Jesus of the Irish Province for students attending Hong Kong University, might

---

[3] Ibid., 397.

be also regarded as a Catholic institution of higher learning. Two Catholic colleges for women were established in 1938, Aurora College for Women and the Women's College of the Catholic University of Peiping, which are treated in the following chapter.[4]

It is to be noted that Catholic institutions of higher learning were restricted to the cities of Peiping, Tientsin, Shanghai, and Hong Kong; and to the provinces of Hopei and Kiangsu, lying along the three great riverways of China. These provinces had become commercially prominent, and were thickly populated. Though the aim of the Catholic missions was to furnish opportunities for religious instruction to as many of China's millions as possible, the missionaries could not force educational programs upon sections of the country wherein such offerings would add little to the welfare of the people.[5]

The increase in enrollment in Catholic institutions of higher learning during the years (1929-39) is indicated in Table XVII.

---

[4]"Catholic Schools in China," Annual of Catholic Missions in China (Peiping, China: Imprimerie des Lazaristes, 1935), p.37.

[5]Thomas Carroll, "The Educational Work of the Catholic Missions in China, 1929-39; A Statistical Survey of the Decade," Digest of Synodal Commission, XIV (January, 1941), 44.

Table XVII

The Enrollment in Catholic Institutions of Higher Learning (1929-39)

Year	Catholics	Non-Catholics	Total
1929-30	151	385	536
1930-31	156	399	555
1931-32	175	638	813
1932-33	194	679	873
1933-34	200	709	909
1934-35	222	839	1,061
1935-36	269	1,030	1,299
1936-37	255	1,137	1,392
1937-38	215	858	1,073
1938-39	311	1,847	2,158
Grand Totals	2,148	8,521	10,669

Aurora University, as mentioned earlier, was the only Catholic institution of higher learning founded up to 1903. This was due to the efforts of Mr. Ma Shang-pei. Shortly afterwards, it was turned over to the direction of the Fathers of the Society of Jesus of the Province of Paris in France.[6] It was at first located at Zikaiwei, but later on was transferred to Dubail Avenue, in the French Settlement of Shanghai. In the beginning, the curriculum of the school was almost entirely modelled on the French pattern of education, and it received generous support from the government of France. In the year 1912, the first

---

[6]Francis A. Rouleau, "Chen Tan: A Chinese Catholic University," America, L (December, 1933), 295.

class of arts and sciences was graduated with twelve students. In 1914, the school of medicine was added to the University.[7]

According to the school report for 1924, the number of professors was 40 and the students 392. By the year 1928, the student body had increased to 450, the staff to 44. At the same time, the library was founded and a new building and a spacious auditorium were erected.[8] Mr. Abel Bonnard wrote of the school in 1927 as follows:

> The professors were all French Jesuits, with the exception of ten laymen who were also French. I had talked with several of the latter, and did not come across one who was not thoroughly keen about his work. I also remember the intense conviction in the manner of Father Henry, the young and charming Rector of the Dawn (Aurora), when he extolled the virtues of some of the young students of the university. He told me that Confucianism had given them extraordinarily well-controlled behavior, wonderful discretion and exquisite delicacy....... At the Dawn one breathed that joyous atmosphere which existed wherever men believed in their work.[9]

In the year 1930, the Heude Museum, which was founded in 1869 by Father Heudein in Zikaiwei, Shanghai, was moved onto the campus. Since then it has been known as the

---

[7]"History of Aurora University," Digest of the Synodal Comission, I (November, 1928), 413-19.

[8]Thomas Carrol, "The Educational Work of the Catholic Missions in China," Digest of Synodal Commission, XIV (March, 1941), 129.

[9]Abel Bonnard, In China (New York: E. P. Dutton & Co., 1927), pp.277-79.

Museum of Natural History of Aurora University. It housed rich botanical and zoological specimens, and contained a unique collection of Chinese antiquities.[10] In 1932, the University was registered with the Ministry of Education under the Chinese name Chen Tan, meaning "dawn" or "Aurora". an imposing collegiste church was built, and a school of dentistry was added in the following year.[11] In 1936, a new five story building, the facade of which was seventeen windows wide, was constructed. A section of this building formed a new library, equipped in most modern fashion and capable of caring for 300,000 volumes.[12]

In 1937, the University maintained three colleges: a college of law, a college of science and engineering, and a college of medicine. It offered four year courses except in medicine which took six years; and conferred degrees equivalent to Licence ès lettres; Licence ès sciences; and docteur en medecine.[13]

The college of law consisted of departments of law,

---

[10] W. Y. Chyne (ed.), Handbook of Cultural Institutions in China (Shanghai, China: Chinese National Committee On Intellectual Co-operation, 1936), p.35.

[11] Digest of the Synodal Commission, VI (January, 1933), 69.

[12] Frank Rawlinson (ed.), The China Christian Yearbook 1936-37 (Glendale, California: Authur H. Clark Co.,1937), p.119.

[13] "Aurora University of Shanghai," Digest of the Synodal Commission, II (December, 1938), 1137.

political and economic sciences. The courses in law were given in French and Chinese. The aim was "to give students a thorough training, and not just a practical knowledge of things."[14] The study was not only of the present codes, but also the history of law and comparative law. The department of political and economic sciences was characterized by a constant adaptation to the geographical, economical and financial problems of the time. It also prepared students for diplomatic careers.[15]

The college of science and engineering was composed of departments of physics and mathematics, electrical engineering, civil engineering, mechanical engineering, and chemical engineering. The laboratories were well-equipped. Each department had a separate building. Its material testing laboratory was well known in Shanghai. Engineers, architects and contractors sent there all kinds of materials to be tested. Many astronomical observatories, bureaus of geodecy, and laboratories often sought out graduates of Aurora for positions in scientific fields. The graduates also enjoyed special privileges at the principal schools of higher technical education in France.[16]

---

[14] *Ibid.*, 1138.
[15] *Ibid.*, 1139.
[16] *Ibid.*, 1140.

Perhaps the best known school was the college of medicine. Considering the number of its students, the merits of its professors and the excellence of the instruction, the college of medicine was among the very finest in China. The students were not alone Chinese, but also Russian, Protuguese, Filipino, French and British youth living in China. The college consisted of (1) a premedical department with faculties of physics, chemistry and natural sciences; (2) a preclinical department with faculties of anatomy, physiology, bateriology, biochemistry and pathology; and (3) two hospitals, St. Anthony's and St. Mary's for clinical training. The faculty was composed of experienced French and Chinese doctors. The moral training of a doctor was regarded as just as important as his scientific formation. Courses of moral philosophy and deontology were conducted by professors whose works on medical ethics were authoritative. All this teaching was condensed in the formula of the oath which the young doctor took before the assembled professors and students on the day he received his degree.[17]

Aurora University was governed by a board of trustees elected according to regulations of the Ministry of Education. The president, rector, and chancellor were

---

[17] *Ibid.*, 1141-43.

appointed by the board of trustees with the approval of the superior of the Society of Jesus in the local Catholic mission. The Status Missionis Shanghai, Societatis Jesu for 1938 contains the following staff statistics, including teachers in the preparatory department: priest of the Society of Jesus 21; scholastics of the Society of Jesus 1; coedjutor Brothers of the Society of Jesus 2; secular priests2; other religious 4; lay leachers 83.

The University occupied a campus of about 20 acres and had 25 buildings for lecture halls, laboratories, auditorium, museum, library, collegiate church, dormitories and faculty residence. The annual income for 1935 was estimated at about CNC$400,263 derived mainly from the Society of Jesus, French Boxer Indemnity Fund, grant from the government of France, student fees, and private donations.[18] The University published Bulletin de L' Université L'Aurora (half-yearly in French); Bulletin Medical (half-yearly, in Chinese and French); Revue Scientifique et Technique (quarterly); Collection du Droit Chinois Modern (18 volumes issued in Chinese and French); and Theses de L'Université L'Aurora (in French.)[19]

---

[18]Ministry of Education, Statistics On Higher Education in China (Shanghai, China: Commercial Press, Ltd.,1938),p.14.
[19]W. Y. Chyne, op. cit., p.34.

Rev. Francis A. Rouleau, S.J. in an article "Chen Tan: A Chinese Catholic University," has paid the following tribute to the Jesuit educators teaching in the school:

> Handling their pupils with sympathetic insight born of long and intimate association with the Chinese people, the Jesuit educators in Shanghai have indeed succeeded, amid the hubhub of the changing political organism and the whirligig of recurrent student discontent, in building up sound traditions of scientific thoroughness and moral discipline that have created for themselves and the University a sterling reputation among the more cultured pagan families of the Republic.[20]

The enrollment in the University over a period of ten years (1929-39) is shown in Table XVIII.

Table XVIII

The Enrollment of Aurora University (1929-39)

Year	Catholics	Non-Catholics	Prep. Dept.	Total
1929-30	65	101	361	527
1930-31	67	117	366	550
1931-32	66	134	328	528
1932-33	70	192	297	559
1933-34	71	231	266	568
1934-35	109	216	311	636
1935-36	122	246	313	681
1936-37	118	277	327	722
1937-38	90	165	360	615
1938-39	129	279	633	1,041
Grand Totls	907	1,958	3,562	6,427

The Tientsin College of Industry and Commerce, popularly known as Hautes Études, was established in September,1923,

---

[20]Francis A. Rouleau, "Chen Tan: A Chinese Catholic University," America, L (December, 1933), 295.

by the Fathers of the Society of Jesus of the Province of Champagne, France. It was opened as a preparatory college with a student body of 50 pupils (Catholic 8, and non-Catholic 42) of which one half were lodged at the College. The classes were conducted at Race Course Road in the British Settlement of the City of Tientsin. On the campus, occupying 23 acres, there were four buildings, one for a lecture hall and three for dormitories.[21] In the year 1925, the college department was formally opened with two faculties, industry and commerce, and with an initial student body of 16 members. During that year, on the staff there were ten Jesuit Fathers. Meanwhile, the Hoangho Paiho Museum of Natural History was founded by the well-known paleontologists, Fathers E. Licent, S.J., and Teilhard de Chardin, S.J. and made a part of the College.[22]

In Jesuit Missions, October, 1930, we find the following comment concerning the school:

> The cause of higher education in China received a new impetus in 1923 with the opening of the University of Tientsin by the Jesuits of the Champagne Province of France. Tientsin is the center of industrial and commercial activity

---

[21]Pascual D'Elia, Catholic Missions in China (Shanghai, China: The Commercial Press, Ltd., 1941), p.57.

[22]Thomas Carrol, "The Educational Work of the Catholic Mission in China," Digest of the Synodal Commission, XIV (March, 1941), 134.

> in Northern China. In keeping with this atmosphere the two most important schools in the University are those of industry and commerce. Attached to the University is the famous Museum Laboratory of Hoangho Pailo established by the well known paleontologists, Fathers Licent, S.J., and Teilhard de Chardin, S.J.[23]

In 1926, a spacious two story building was erected, with two wings, each 31 meters long, one for a large chapel and the other for a library. The central part of the new building was for classrooms, laboratories, and administrative offices.[24] By 1927, the student body increased to 90 members of which one-third were Catholic. At the same time, the faculty comprised 11 Jesuit Fathers, 6 Chinese lay professors and 11 European lay teachers. In the year 1930, the college preparatory department was abolished and replaced by a senior middle school. Reverend George de Jonghe, M.E.P. in his quarterly letter in Fides in 1931, dealing with Catholic education in China, mentioned this College as follows:

> The Catholic University of Tientsin (Hautes Etudes) opened its term (1931) with 120 students The modest figure is explained by the difficult entrance qualifications, the strict discipline,

---

23"Jesuit Mission Vignettes," Jesuit Missions, IV (October, 1930), 211.

24"Les Hautes Etudes, Tientsin," Digest of the Synodal Commission , II (February, 1929), 80.

> and the policy of obtaining positions for all graduates. Jesuit traditions are evident in the institution, and it needs but a few hours' inspection to see the perfect order and the high choice of students. Especially impressive is the strong piety of the Christian groups.[25]

By 1932, the enrollment increased to 364 students (124 Catholic and 240 non-Catholic). In August, 1933, the school was officially approved by the Ministry of Education under the Chinese name, Tientsin Kung Shang College, with schools of engineering and commerce.[26] In September, 1937, two new departments, architectural engineering, and imports and exports were added. In that same year, the laboratories were greatly enlarged and a new one for heat engines installed. Rev. René Charvet,S.J., was appointed rector in 1938.[27]

The College offered four year courses leading to bachelor degrees in engineering and commerce. The school of engineering consisted of departments of civil, mechanical, and architectural engineering; while the school of commerce consisted of departments of business administration,

---

[25]George de Jonghe, "Catholic Education in China," Jesuit Missions, V (April, 1931), 96.

[26]Ministry of Education, The Second China Educational Yearbook (Shanghai, China: The Commercial Press, Ltd., 1948), p.237.

[27]Frank Rawlinson, op. cit., p.119.

finance and accounting, and imports and exports.[28] According to the constitution of the College, the object of the school of engineering was to "to provide a thorough course of training for public works, railway construction, hydraulics, building construction, and drafting topography." The object of the school of commerce was:

> To provide a thoroughly practical and up-to-date training for the following professions: commercial managers of industrial or trading concerns; chartered accountants; experts in various raw products and factory and plant management; competent export and import traders; bankers; brokers; and insurance agents; and men of comprehensive outlook; familiar with the main philosophical and social problems; and qualified to occupy prominent positions in social and public life.[29]

Tientsin College was governed by the local Catholic Church authorities. However, most of the administrative staff and many professors were members of the Society of Jesus of the Champagne Province in France.[30] The school was well-equipped with research facilities. There were laboratories for testing commodities and materials; likewise for physics; chemistry; hydraulics; soil mechanics;

---

[28]Ministry of Education, op. cit., p.238.

[29]"The Constitution of the Tientsin University," Digest of the Synodal Commission, II (February, 1929), 88-89.

[30]M. M. Chambers (ed.), Universities of the World Outside U.S.A. (Washington, D.C.: American Council On Education, 1950), p.237.

heat engineering; metallography; electrical engineering; also a machine shop; a woodworking shop; a foundry; a forge; and ample surveying equipment.[31] The Hoangho Paiho Museum of Natural History; located on the campus, contained many specimens from the area of North China. The exhibits in the museum were related to the department of geology, paleontology and rock industries, and the department of botany, zoology and anthropology.[32]

The annual budget for 1935-36 was estimated at about CNC$215,000 for income and CNC$204,840 as expenses. The sources of the income were mainly from the Society of Jesus, student fees, and private donations.[33] The college library contained a total of 55,000 volumes (Chinese, 21,369; Western, 33,631.) Among the college publications were Tao Kung Weekly (in Chinese); Journal of Engineering and Commerce (half-yearly); Collection "Le Droit Chinois Modern" (in French); Economic Studies (in English or French); and Collection sur L'Histoire des Sciences en Chine (in Franch)[34]

The enrollment of the College from 1929 to 1939 is given in Table XIX.

---

[31] *Ibid.*, p.238.
[32] W. Y. Chyne, *op. cit.*, p.115.
[33] Ministry of Education, *Statistics On Higher Education in China*, p.16.
[34] W. Y. Chyne, *op. cit.*, p.109.

Table XIX

The Enrollment of Tientsin College of Industry and Commerce (1929-39)

Year	Catholics	Non-Catholics	Prep. Dept.	Total
1929-30	17	50	50	117
1930-31	12	51	60	123
1931-32	8	46	217	271
1932-33	19	38	307	364
1933-34	21	74	445	540
1934-35	37	86	490	613
1935-36	34	105	414	553
1936-37	33	108	314	455
1937-38	40	120	544	704
1938-39	55	265	706	1026
Grand Totals	276	943	3547	4766

In July, 1912, Mr. Vincent Ying and Mr. Ma Shang-pei, envisioning greater support for the spread of the Faith in China through the establishment of a Catholic University at Peking, addressed a letter to His Holiness Pope Pius X, which expressed the need and the advantage of such an institution. It read in part:

> While the Protestants of England, Germany and America are building schools and universities, we note with sorrow that the Catholic Missions alone remain indifferent to the educational movement. In this capital of China, the Catholics have no university; no secondary schools; not even primary schools.......
>
> A Catholic university here would see large numbers of students, both Christian and pagan, flocking to its doors; it would constitute a strong bond of union between Catholicity and and the nation at large........

> From the bottom of our hearts, we implore you, our Father and Teacher, to have pity upon us and to send us missionaries, virtuous and learned, to found in this great capital a university open alike to Christians and pagans, a university that will be a model proposed to the entire nation, preparing an elite among Catholics and bringing true enlightenment to pagans.[35]

In 1913, Mr. Ying instituted at Hsiang Shan near Peking the Fu Jen She, an academy of Chinese letters for Catholic young men. In 1918, he was obliged to suspend the work of this academy because of inadequate funds. This was ultimately to be revived, however, as the MacManus Academy of Chinese Studies.[36] In the year 1919, His Holiness Pope Benedict XV appointed a commission to study the possibilities of establishing a Catholic university at Peking. Later on the project was taken up by His Holiness Pope Pius XI, who through a letter of His Eminence, Cardinal William Van Rossum , Prefect of the Sacred Congregation of the Propaganda, urged the American Cassinese Congregation of Benedictines to undertake the founding of the school.

---

[35]Vincent Ying Lien-chih, "Letter to Pope Pius X," Bulletin of the Catholic University of Peking, I (Sept., 1926), 35-37.

[36]"Chronicle of Events Connected with the Origin of the Catholic University of Peking," Bulletin of the Catholic University of Peking, I (September, 1926), 63.

> It is the most intense desire of this Sacred Congregation that the Order of St. Benedict, which during the Middle Ages saved Latin and Greek literature from certain destruction, should found in the city of Peking an institute of higher Chinese studies as the most apt means of fostering a more vigorous growth of our Holy Religion in the vast territory of China.[37]

In August, 1923, the American Cassinese Congregation of Benedictines held a meeting in the Abbey of St. Procopius at Lisle, Illinois, concerning the proposal of the Cardinal Prefect of the Propaganda, and finally voted to accept the responsibility. St. Vincent Archabbey, Latrobe, Pennsylvania, was chosen as consignee, with the promise of support, both moral and physical, on the part of all the other abbeys of the Congregation.[38] In 1925, the Rt. Rev. Aurelius Stehle, O.S.B., Archabbot of St. Vincent, and Rev. George Barry O'Toole, Obl.S.B., D.D. were appointed by the Holy See as Chancellor and Rector of the Catholic University of Peking respectively. In February of the same year they arrived in China. By the fall of that year, the estate of Prince Tsai Tao was purchased and steps were immediately taken to renovate the buildings and

---

[37]"Catholic University of Peking," Catholic World CXXIX (June, 1929), 343.

[38]"Chronicle of Events Connected with the Origin of the Catholic University of Peking," Bulletin of the Catholic University of Peking, I (September, 1926), 64.

to convert them into a school. In the meantime a preparatory school - the MacManus Academy - was opened. It was so named because of the generous benefactions of Mr. Theodore MacManus, LL.D., of Detroit, Michigan which made the opening of the school possible.[39]

By 1926, the student body had rapidly increased. It was then decided to establish a board of trustees and to raise the academy to the status of a university under the Chinese name Fu Jen University,[40] with Dr. George Barry O'Toole and Mr Chen Yuan as its president and vice-president respectively. The University, which then consisted of only a college of arts and letters, was duly recognized by the provincial government in the following year.

At that time there were 150 students, of whom 65 were Catholics. The school had 24 teachers and officials, of whom 15 were Chinese laymen and 9 were American Benedictine

---

39"Catholic University of Peking," Catholic Digest, IV (February, 1940), 74.

40The two words, Fu Jen, are taken from a sentence in the 24th chapter of Book XII of Confucius' Analects: "Chun-tse i wen hui yu fu jen;" which is translated by Legge as: "The superior man on grounds of culture meets with his friends, and by their friendship helps his virtue." Hence the selection of the two characters, Fu Jen (promotion of righteousness) is in accord with the Chinese custom of taking one or two essential words from a classical passage to convey the complete meaning of that passage; and it conveys to the Chinese mind the threehold ideal of perfection in the intellectual, the moral and the social order.

Fathers.[41] The local newspaper, Shu Tien Shih Pao, June 7, 1927, gave the following account of the foundation:

> Two years ago the American Benedictines bought Tao Pei-le's Palace outside the Hou Men for the purpose of establishing a Catholic University. Their aim is to preserve the culture and literature of China. They have invited Mr. Chen Yuan, former Vice-Minister of Education, to act as (Chinese) president and have changed the title of the University to Fu Jen. They have already applied to the Department of Education for registration. The said university comprises four departments, namely, the departments of Chinese, English, history and archaeology, and philosophy. Applicants are being accepted for the next scholastic year.[42]

In 1929, two more colleges were added, natural sciences and education. The board of trustees was, however, reorganized as required by the Ministry of Education with a majority of Chinese members and Mr. Chen Yuan was appointed president.[43] In the following year, a new building designed in Chinese architecture by the famous Benedictine architect Dom Adelbert Gresnight, O.S.B., was completed. It was a massive building in four green-tiled corner towers with the central roof covering the auditorium. The building accomodiated a library, an auditorium, offices, and a

---

41 "Catholic University of Peking," Digest of the Synodal Commission, II (May, 1929), 350.

42 Shun Tien Shih Pao (Shun Tien Daily News), June 7, 1927, 3.

43 Digest of the Synodal Commission, V (October, 1932), 926.

dormitory sufficient to house 400 students.[44] In 1931, the University had its first graduation with 78 graduates. At the same time the Ministry of Education granted the school permanent registration. Dom Francis Clougherty, O.S.B, was appointed by the Holy See as the new chancellor. In 1932, a summer school was conducted on the campus with 34 students including secular priests, religious, and laymen from different provinces attending courses and special lectures.[45]

However, during the depression in the United States, the American Cassinese Congregation of the Benedictine Order found it very difficult to maintain the University. Archbishop Celso Constantini, then Apostolic Delegate to China, went to the United States and made known its financial distress to the Seventh National Convention of the Catholic Students' Mission Crusade at Niagara University. The Convention pledged its best effort to aid the University.[46] Later in 1933, the Holy See transferred the University to the care of the Society of the

---

[44] "A Sino-Christian Architecture," Digest of the Synodal Commission, II (May, 1929), 350.

[45] "University News," Fu Jen Magazine, I (September, 1932), 25-26.

[46] "Catholic University of Peiping," Catholic Digest, IV (February, 1940), 75.

Divine Word. The Very Rev. Joseph Grendel, S.T.D., then Superior-General of the Society was appointed chancellor and Very Rev. Joseph Murphy, S.V.D. became rector.[47]

In 1934, postgraduate courses in physics and history leading to the M.A. degree after two years' work were offered. There was an initial enrollment of four students, of whom three were Catholics.[48] In 1935, the University celebrated the tenth anniversary of its founding. At that time there were 749 students not including 219 pupils in the preparatory course. With the death of Very Rev. Joseph Murphy, S.V.D., the Rev. Rudoph Rahmann, S.V.D. was appointed rector.[49]

The Catholic University of Peking was the only pontifical institution in China. The chancellor and rector were appointed directly by and responsible to the Holy Father. It was governed by a board of trustees with fifteen members. There was also an administrative staff, a university senate, an executive council, and an academic council.[50] According to the statement of Les Missions Catholiques de Chine in 1938, the personnel of the University

---

47 Year Book of Catholic University of Peking, 1948, p.2.
48 "University News," Fu Jen Magazine, II (Jan., 1934), 25.
49 Digest of the Synodal Commission, X (Jan., 1937), 66.
50 Catalogue of the Catholic University of Peking, 1947-1948, pp.23-31.

included 22 priests, 4 Brothers and 116 lay professors.[51]

In his message to the faculty and student body as the new rector in 1934, the Very Rev. Joseph Murphy, S.V.D., stated the aims of the University as follows:

> The University aims to assist in deepening the cultural life of our Catholics in every way in China. We need teachers thoroughly trained for our own schools, we need priests trained not merely in Western literature and not merely by Western men, but trained completely also in their own culture fundamentally and trained by the best scholars of their own race. We need a center in the North of China where Catholic principles are exposed and defended in all the branches of modern science, where scientific training of the best type can be given to our Catholic students. We need Catholic scholars capable of studying and explaining the treasures of Chinese literature and history, treasures which reach back three thousand years, and especially, do we need scholars who are capable of explaining the treasures of the glorious periods of Ricci and the Jesuits in the 16th century.[52]

The University in 1936 consisted of three colleges: (1) a college of arts and letters with departments of Chinese language and literature; Western languages and literature; history; social sciences (sociology and economics); (2) a college of sciences with departments of mathematics; physics; chemistry; biology; pharmacy; and a premedical

---

[51] Les Missions Catholiques de Chine, 1938, p.35.

[52] Joseph Murphy, "Message of the New Rector," Fu Jen Magazine, II (January, 1934), 3-5.

course; and (3) a college of education with departments of pedagogy; philosophy and psychology; home economics; and fine arts. It offered four year courses and conferred bachelor degrees in arts, sciences and education. In addition, it provided postgraduate courses in physics and history leading to the M.A. degree.[53]

The University maintained a museum and operated a university press. Its laboratories were well-equipped for research facilities in physics, chemistry, biology and psychology. The Institute of Microbiology, founded by Rev. Joseph Rutten, C.I.C.M., and the only institute in the Far East producing typhus vaccine, was taken over by the University in 1936. The department of fine arts developed Chinese Christian art and used Christian ideas as the inspiration for many fine paintings. This department owed its origin to the former Apostolic Delegate to China, Archbishop Constantini, who advocated the use of native art as a means of spreading the Faith. The department also designed altars, liturgical emblems, church ornamentation, murals, chalices and patens of cloisonné, all in Chinese style.[54]

---

[53] _Catalogue of the Catholic University of Peking, 1936-1937_, pp.42-58.

[54] "Catholic University of Peking," _Digest of the Synodal Commission_, X (January, 1937), 70.

The annual budget for the academic year 1935-36 was estimated at about CNC$338,845 for income and CNC$326,678 for expenses. The sources of income were derived mainly from the Sacred Congregation of Propaganda, the Society of the Divine Word, student fees, government grants, and private donations.[55] The library contained approximately 94,398 Chinese volumes and 34,046 volumes in Western languages.[56] The University published three Sinological periodicals: (1) The Fu Jen Sinological Journal (semi-annually in Chinese); (2) Monumenta Serica (semi-annually in English, French, and German); and (3) Folklore Studies, (annually in English, French, and German). A fourth periodical, Fu Jen Magazine published in Chicago, kept friends and benefactors in the United States informed of the school's progress.[57]

In January, 1940, The Shield (organ of the Catholic Students Mission Crusade in the United States) made the following comment concerning the school:

55Ministry of Education (ed.), Statistics On Education in China (Shanghai, China: The Commercial Press, Ltd., 1938), p.14.

56Ministry of Education, The Second China Educational Yearbook, p.165.

57Catholic University of Peking, Yearbook of the Catholic University of Peking, 1948 (Peiping, China: Catholic University Press, 1948), p.2.

> Besides providing courses in the arts and sciences to future Catholic lay leaders of China, Fu Jen University is performing a number of other services for the establishment of Christian culture. First in importance, perhaps, is the service which it has provided for the native clergy, number of whom have come to the University for post-ordination courses, enabling them to exercise greater influence among the educated classes.
>
> Of great importance, too, is the increased prestige of the Catholic Church which the University has effected through its non-Catholic graduates. Among the 672 students who have been graduated, there have been only 121 Catholics. But the others will carry with them a friendliness for the Catholic way of life, and this attitude will affect the future.[58]

Since the establishment of a Catholic institution of higher learning in China was a major project, the Catholic Missions could not afford many such institutions. For this reason, the Plenary Council of Shanghai in 1924 made a pronouncement in favor of Catholic hostels in connection with non-Catholic or secular institutions of higher learning in order to safeguard the faith and morals of Catholic students.[59] In November, 1928, the conerstone of the first Catholic hostel, known as Ricci Hall, was laid by the Fathers of the Society of Jesus of the

---

[58] "Catholic University of Peking," The Shield, IV (January, 1940), 13.

[59] I. L. Kandel (ed.), "Roman Catholic Agencies in China," Educational Yearbook, 1933 (New York: International Institute of the Columbia University, 1933), p.579.

Irish Province for students attending Hong Kong University.[60] It was modeled after the well known Campion Hall of Oxford in England. The Hall was completed and opened for students in the following year. The aim of the founding of this hostel was "to give special tutoring in scholastic subjects to the students of Hong Kong University and, at the same time, to add a Catholic atmosphere to the educational environment."[61] Besides educational services in Ricci Hall, several of the Jesuit Fathers occupied professorial chairs in Hong Kong University itself. During the period, 1929-39, a total of 503 students were housed in Ricci Hall, of whom 235 were Catholics and 268 were non-Catholics.[62] Similar hostels were planned by other religious orders, such as Nanking Institute, which was to be in charge of the American Jesuits of California in Nanking for students attending the National Central University.[63]

---

[60]"New Hostel for University," Digest of the Synodal Commission, II (January, 1929), 22.

[61]Thomas Carrol, "The Educational Work of the Catholic Missions in China," Digest of the Synodal Commission, XIV (March, 1941), 139.

[62]Thomas Carrol, "A Statistical Survey of the Decade of the Catholic Educational Work in China," Digest of the Synodal Commission, XIV (January, 1941), 45.

[63]Rock Magazine (Shanghai, China: Rock Magazine Press, 1937), V (April, 1937), 224.

It was not unusual for Catholic missioners to teach in secular universities. Fr. John Rurner, S.J. of the Irish Province was offered a position as lecturer by the University authorities at Sun Yat-sen University in Canton. Fr. Canice Egan, S.J. became professor of English in Chu Hai University; Fr. Richard Kennedy, S.J. held the same position in the University of Canton; and Fr. Edmond Sullivan, S.J. taught at Chung Hsu University. Two Maryknoll Fathers, Fr. Joseph Hahn, M.M., and Fr. George Putnam, M.M., taught in the departments of engineering and sociology respectively at Lingnan University. The Maryknoll Society built a commodious house with a chapel annexed to it on the campus of Lingnan University. The Fathers used this building not only for religious instructions, but also as a center of Catholic social life for university students both Catholic and non-Catholic.[64]

Summary

The educational work of the Catholic Church in China extended over the whole country and included the three levels: elementary, secondary, and higher. Before the

---

[64]Thomas R. Fitzgerald, "Missioners in Secular Universities," China Missionary Bulletin, I (March, 1949), 255.

Sino-Japanese War (1937), the Church maintained about 14,00 schools with almost a half million pupils. However, Catholic missionary work emphasized the apostolate among the masses and educational efforts were principally devoted to the poor and underprivileged. Consequently, there were only three Catholic institutions of higher learning in China and one hostel for students attending Hong Kong University. These were Aurora University in Shanghai; Tientsin College of Industry and Commerce; Fu Jen, the Catholic University of Peking; and Ricci Hall at Hong Kong University. In 1937, there were 1,392 students in the four institutions, of whom 255 were Catholics and 1,137 were pagans. There were approximately 300 staff members in all.

Aurora University at Shanghai was the only Catholic institution of higher learning founded before the Republic. It was under the management of the Fathers of the Society of Jesus of the Province of Paris in France. Its curriculum was modelled on the French pattern of education and led to the French degrees of _licence ès lettres_ and _licence ès sciences_. The French language was the medium of instruction in the University. Among the three colleges of medicine, law, and engineering and sciences, the school of medicine had the largest enrollment. The graduate of the three colleges were distinguished throughout China.

The Heude Museum of Natural History of Aurora University, which housed rich botanical and zoological collections, was one of the finest of its kind in the Far East.

Tientsin College of Industry and Commerce, known as Hautes Études, was founded in 1923 by the Jesuits of the Province of Champagne, France. It specialized in industry and commerce. Its laboratories were well-equipped with research facilities for further study in physics and chemistry. The famous Museum of Hoangho Pailo, which was attached to the College, contained valuable specimens for the study of geology, palaeontology, botany, zoology, and anthropology.

The Catholic University of Peiping, founded in 1925, was the realization of a plan fostered by the Holy See for an institution of higher learning in Peiping, the cultural capital of China, after a petition for such a school was presented to the Holy Father by Mr. Vincent Ying and Mr. Ma Shang-pei. It was first entrusted to the American Cassinese Congregation of Benedictines. After 1933 it was transferred to the Society of the Divine Word. The University had a deserving reputation for courses in literature and the sciences. Its school of art spread Christian ideas throughout the nation. It had an imposing group of buildings in Chinese architecture which were one of the chief tourist attractions in a city of great palaces and magnificent temples.

Ricci Hall of Hong Kong was founded in 1929 by the Jesuits of the Irish Province for students attending Hong Kong University. It aimed to safeguard the faith and morals of Catholic students as well as to give special tutoring in scholastic subjects. Similar hostels were planned by other religious orders in cities near secular universities. It was not unusual for missioners to teach in secular universities, because by doing they were carrying the work of the apostolate among university students.

Chapter IV

Further Growth and Development of Privately Controlled Higher Education (1937-48)

The year 1937 marked the outbreak of the Sino-Japanese War which greatly affected the development of higher education in China. Before the war, there were in China 108 institutions of higher learning including 53 private schools. By the end of 1937, the number of institutions dropped to 91; while private schools were reduced to 47. Many of these institutions were destroyed or seriously damaged by the Japanese.[1]

During the war, the cultural center of China shifted from the North and the East Coast to the western provinces. Cities like Kunming, Kweiyang, Chungking and Chengtu became new seats of higher learning. Most of these refugee institutions in the interior suffered from lack of adequate buildings and other facilities. Classes were held in the old temples or private homes. The faculty and student body were seriously hindered in their efforts. However, several nondenominational institutions still remained in the occupied

---

[1]Library Association of China; A Survey of Higher Education in China During the War (Peiping, China: Library Association of China, 1938), p.18.

areas, viz., Peiping and Shanghai.[2]

Due to the tendency toward regimentation and centralization in school administration, the universities of Fuh Tan, Nankai, Amoy, and Hsiang Ya Medical College became national institutions under the control and support of the Chinese Central Government. A notable experiment was undertaken in the organization of the so-called "Federated Universities," or "Associated Colleges" by combing existing institutions in the interior, such as Southwestern Associated University in Kunming.[3]

Despite the war, the number of institutions of higher learning apparently increased. According to the Ministry of Education, in 1948, there were 207 universities, colleges and professional schools, of which 79 were private. From 1937 to 1948, thirty-four private institutions of higher learning were founded; of these 32 were nondenominational, and 2 were Catholic. Of the 32 recently founded nondenominational institutions, four were universities; twelve were colleges; and sixteen were professional schools.[4]

---

[2]Chen Yuan, "Universities in China; a great migration," New York Times: Educational Supplement (July 21, 1945), 340.

[3]Li-fu Chen, Chinese Education During the War (Chungking, China: Ministry of Education, 1942), p.15.

[4]Ministry of Education, The Second China Educational Yearbook, 1948, (Shanghai, China: The Kai-ming Book Co., 1948), p.1406.

Figure I

Nationalist School System

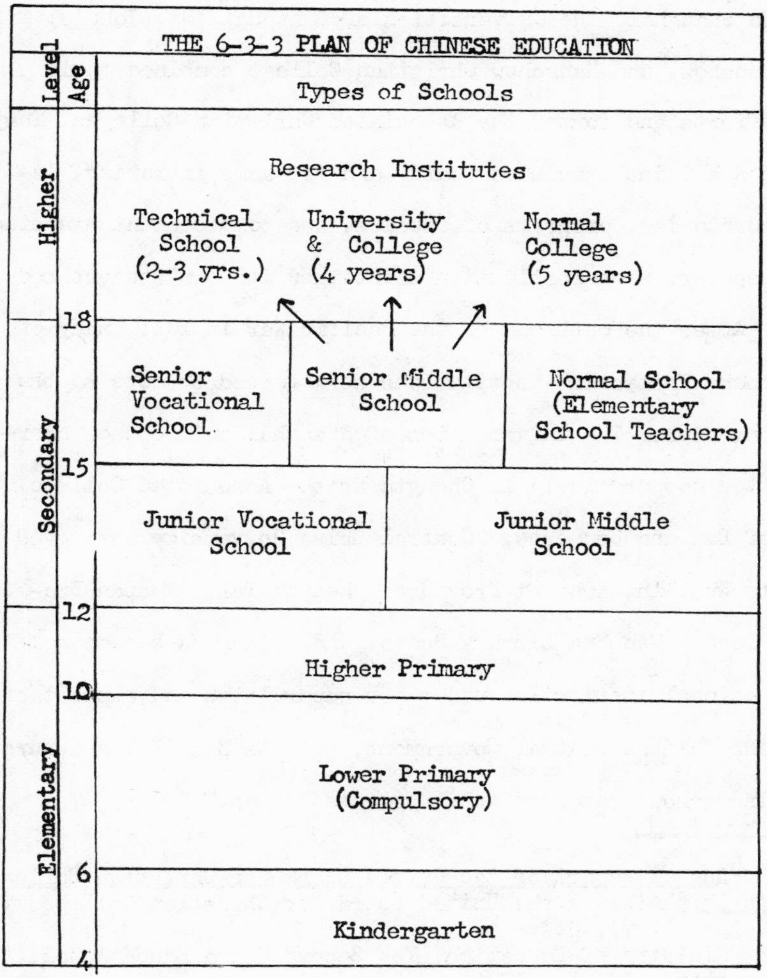

THE 6-3-3 PLAN OF CHINESE EDUCATION

Level	Age	Types of Schools		
Higher		Research Institutes		
		Technical School (2-3 yrs.)	University & College (4 years)	Normal College (5 years)
Secondary	18	Senior Vocational School	Senior Middle School	Normal School (Elementary School Teachers)
	15	Junior Vocational School	Junior Middle School	
Elementary	12	Higher Primary		
	10	Lower Primary (Compulsory)		
	6	Kindergarten		
	4			

Among the Protestant institutions, the universities of Nanking, Cheeloo, Yenching and Soochow, and Ginling College for Women were moved to Chengtu, where they joined West China Union University; and became associated universities. In Shanghai, the universities of Shanghai, St. John's, Soochow, and Hangchow Christian College combined their efforts and formed the Associated Christian Colleges. They had a joint executive board, and the same libraries, laboratories, programs of studies, and commencement exercises. However, each institution maintained its own student body.[5]

After the outbreak of the Pacific War in 1941, many of these Protestant institutions were forced to move to the interior. The universities of Shanghai and Soochow operated cooperatively in Chengtu as the Associated College of Law and Commerce. Central China University was moved to Kweilin, Kwangsi Province; then to Tali, Yunnan Province. Wen Hua Library School and Hsiang Ya became a national institution under the supervision and support of the Chinese Central Government, but its hospital and nursing school retained their private status.[6]

---

[5]Annual Report of the United Board for Christian Colleges in China (New York: United Board for Christian Colleges in China, 1939), p.4.

[6]Ministry of Education, The Second China Educational Yearbook, 1948, p.177.

In the South, Fukien Christian University and Hua Nan College for Women were moved to Shaowu and Nanping, Fukien Province, respectively.[7] Lingnan University shifted its teaching activities to temporary accommodations on the campus of Hong Kong University. When Hong Kong was occupied by the Japanese in 1941, the University was forced to move to Kukiang, Kwangtung Province. After the war was over, these Protestant institutions returned to their former campuses.[8]

Postwar rehabilitation problems made the executive boards of Protestant institutions realize the necessity of a closer cooperative relationship in order to obtain the best results with limited financial resources and personnel. Accordingly the United Boards for Christian Colleges in China, the British Christian Universities Association, and the Council of Higher Education of the Christian Colleges Association set up a planning commission to study postwar conditions of higher education in China. They made significant suggestions concerning the reorganization of Protestant institutions of higher learning. It was decided that

---

[7]Ministry of Education, Summary Review of the Institutions of Higher Learning in China, p.403.

[8]Ministry of Education, The Second China Educational Yearbook, 1948, p.168.

Protestant institutions should be combined into nine schools and located in the following centers: Peiping, Shanghai, Nanking, Canton, Foochow and Central China. However, this plan could not be successfully carried out because of the Communist control of China from 1949 to the present.[9]

During the war, the Catholic institutions of higher learning remained on their own campuses and carried on as usual. Aurora University continued its work on the campus in the French Concession of Shanghai, and the Franch Jesuits did exceptional service for the nation in keeping learning alive on the "Isolated Island."[10] Tientsin College of Industry and Commerce (Hautes Études) remained in Tientsin and the student body gradually increased. It was raised to the status of a university in 1947, and its name changed to Tsinku University.[11] The Catholic University of Peiping continued to operate on its own campus in Peiping. The Ecclesiastical Institute for Chinese priests, a graduate school of arts and sciences, and a museum for oriental

---

9"The Report of the Council of Higher Education of Christian Colleges Association in China in 1947," Lingnan University Bulletin, LI (April, 1947), 1-3.

10China Missionary Bulletin, I (1948), 109.

11Ibid., 869.

ethnology were established in the University during this period.[12]

Two Catholic institutions for women - Aurora College for Women and the Women's College of the Catholic University of Peiping - were founded in 1938. The former was under the direction of the Sisters of the Society of the Sacred Heart, and had departments of arts and sciences; the latter was established by the Society of the Divine Word, and entrusted to the Sisters Servants of the Holy Ghost. It maintained departments of arts and letters, education, agriculture, and sciences.[13]

At a session of the National Catholic Educational Congress held at Aurora College for Women in Shanghai, in February, 1948, Cardinal Tien delivered an address in which he made suggestions for improving the program of Catholic education in China. Special proposals for the expansion of Catholic higher education were adopted. However, they could not be put into effect because of the advent of the Communist regime.[14]

---

[12] "Annual Report of the Catholic University of Peiping, 1939-40," Digest of the Synodal Commission, XIII (Dec., 1940), 990-96.

[13] Thomas Carrol, S.J., "The Educational Work of the Catholic Mission in China, 1929-39," Digest of the Synodal Commission, XIV (June, 1941), 528.

[14] John B. Kao, "National Catholic Educational Congress, February 15-21, 1948," China Missionary Bulletin, II (1948), 149.

Table XXVII

Enrollment Of Catholic Institutions of Higher Learning (1945)

Institutions	Locations	Religious in Charge	Student Body
Aurora University	Shanghai	French Jesuits	1,748
Aurora College for Women	Shanghai	Sisters of Society of Sacred Heart	848
Tsinku (Hautes Etudes) University	Tientsin	French Jesuits	1,900
Catholic University of Peiping	Peiping	Society of the Divine Word	1,899
Women's College of the Catholic University of Peiping	Peiping	Sisters Servants of Holy Ghost	1,465
Ricci Hall of Hong Kong	Hong Kong	Irish Jesuits	*

Map II: Locations Of Privately Controlled Institutions Of Higher Learning During the Sino-Japanese War. Shaded area indicates territory occupied by the Japanese.

Chapter V

The Status of Private Higher Education Under Communist Control (1949-53)

A. Communist Educational Policy and the Reorganization of Higher Education

After a war of eight years, China finally defeated her enemy, Japan, from without. Meanwhile the peril of Communism was increasing from within. The Chinese Communists took advantage of postwar unsettled conditions to spread their influence throughout the nation. By 1949, Communism almost controlled completely the whole State, and forced the Kuomintang Government to withdraw from the mainland to Taiwan (Formosa), an island east of Fukien Province. The so-called People's Central Government was then established at Peiping with Mao Tse-tung as president.

Under the Communist regime education is the function of the State. All education must be controlled by the government. Private schools have a recognized status, but they, the same as government schools, are controlled by the government. This control is exercised over courses, textbooks, schedules, holidays, tuition fees and staff. All college graduates are required to put themselves at the service of the government. The Soviet educational system as well as its teaching methods have been adopted.

University and college courses extend from three to five years, and specialized higher studies from two to three years. The periods of study, however, are not fixed mechanically; the objectives of the prescribed courses are the important consideration.[1]

Objectives of Higher Education

Communistic education means the teaching of Communist principles and the Communist philosophy of life. Education must be nationalized, popularized and largely scientific. Education is for all the people, especially the laboring class, and not for any one particular class. The emphasis is on numbers rather than on standards. The main task of higher education is to train personnel for national reconstruction. A materialistic outlook and the scientific method must prevail in the schools. China is to be transformed from an agriculturally backward nation into a modern industrialized country. For this reason, science, engineering, agriculture, and medicine are given priority. The new regime has indicated disapproval of law departments in universities, and has prohibited the teaching of theology and religion. Education must be definitely

---

[1]Department of State (ed.), People's Handbook (Shanghai, China: Ta Kung Pao, 1952), p.452.

political and lead the student to an understanding and appreciation of the great proletarian revolution.[2]

School Administration

Changes in school administration are among the more radical educational developments. Students Self-Governing Associations have been organized in most institutions of higher learning and given a voice in many aspects of administration. In each school there is also a teachers' union and workingmen's union. Administrative committees, representing professors, instructors, staff members, students, and laborers, are set up in colleges and universities. They participate in formulating educational policies, and in managing school affairs. The position of dean of discipline has been abolished.[3] The proof of the practicability of such school administration is based on the fact that the universities of Peking, Tsinghua, and Yenching have been virtually without a president for sometime, but this has not interfered with their normal functions.[4]

---

[2]Ministry of Education (ed.), The Cultural and Educational Policy Adopted by The Chinese People's Consultative Conference in 1949 (Peiping, China: Sin-hua Book Co., 1949), p.194.

[3]Ibid., p.196.

[4]"Some New Educational Developments in China," China Weekly Review, CXIV (September, 1949), 37.

Figure II

Present School System of China

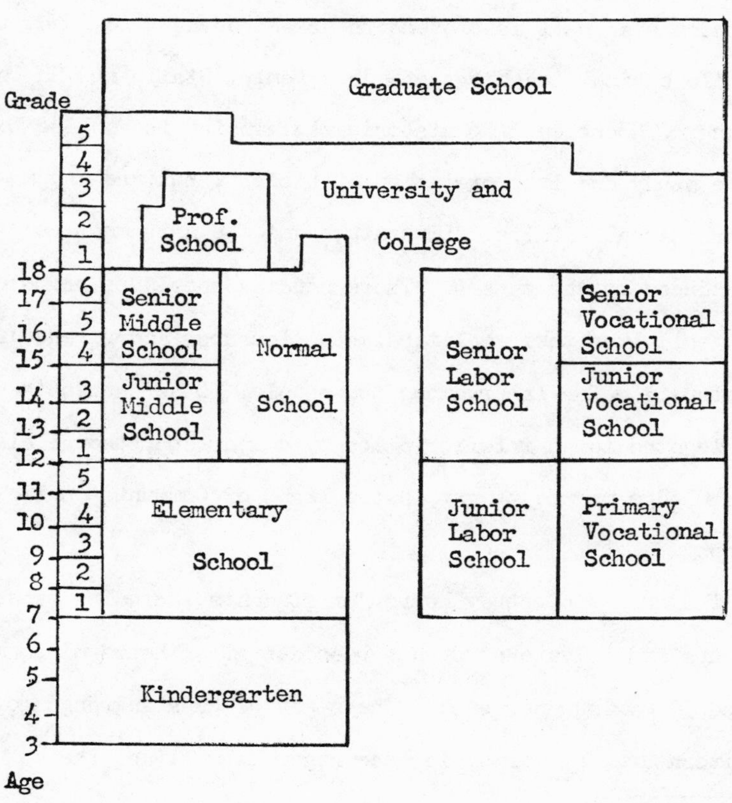

Data taken from People's Handbook, Shanghai, China: Ta-kung-pao Press, 1952. P.453.

Curriculum

Courses for colleges and universities have been shortened and are largely practical. Political science according to the principles of historical and dialectical materialism is required for all students. Marxist economics have in general replaced the traditional courses in economics. Students as well as professors are encouraged to study the philosophical teachings of Marx, Lenin, Stalin and Ma Tse-tung. The scientific historical viewpoint is applied to the study and interpretation of history, culture and international affairs. Literature and the arts must be produced by the masses. These studies should be promoted to enlighten their political consciousness and to encourage enthusiasm for labor among the people. Other subjects are relegated to an inferior place by comparison, though all knowledge may be taught in the light of Communist philosophy.[5]

The number of study hours for students including experiments and private study has been set at 44 hours minimum and 50 maximum per week. The study of Russian language, literature, and arts, is encouraged as well as the

---

[5]Mao Tse-tung, "Reform Our Learning," Maoism (A source book for the writings of Mao Tse-tung), (Hong Kong: Sinhua Book Co., 1949), p.801.

imitation of Soviet cultural and educational practices. A committee has been appointed by the Ministry of Education of the People's Central Government to translate Russian college textbooks for use in Chinese schools.[6]

Teaching Methods

The methods of education aim to unify theory and practice. Learning and practical work are of equal importance. In teaching, emphasis is placed on discussion and on inducing students to study for themselves. Classes are supposed to investigate practical problems, and in many cases students combine their study with periods of practical work in government organizations. Both teachers and students are expected to join in actual productive labor in order to break down the traditional separation between mental and manual work. Special emphasis is placed upon the training of workers for public service in mines, industry, financial and information centers.[7]

Learning is imparted in "Small Mutual-help Group", "Big Class," and "Discussion Groups." Each "Small Mutual-help Group" consists of ten to twelve members, led by a

---

[6]Michael Lindsay (ed.), Notes on Educational Problems in Communist China (New York: International Secretariat Institute of Pacific Relations, 1950), p.192.

[7]Ibid., p.194.

Communist teacher. Study books are selected from Communist literature or articles and reports from Communist leaders on current events. In these small groups criticism and self-criticism are encouraged. Every member must take part in the discussion, thus revealing his thinking. If his viewpoint is unacceptable, he is at first warned and then exhorted to change his opinions. If he remains obdurate, he is discriminated against and sent to the "Big Class."[8]

The "Big Class" is nothing more than a center of coercion and indoctrination. The teacher, always a Communist, lectures on the theories and principles of Marxism and Leninism and the selected writings of Mao Tse-tung. Students who do not change their minds or raise questions contrary to what is taught are classified as reactionaries. The names of these students are taken down by the teacher and later on circulated among the "Discussion Group", in which they are literally mentally tortured until they lose courage to raise further questions of the same nature. They are discriminated against in daily life until they find themselves in an impossible position; and either

---

[8]"Education in Communist China," World Today, VIII (June, 1950), 257-68.

capitulate or are crushed.[9]

Activity Program

Aside from teaching, the government has appointed special teachers to undertake the organization of extracurricular activity programs. There is in each school also an official youth organization called "New Democracy Youth Fellowship" for the purpose of promoting party programs, discussing Communist doctrines, and opposing reactionary tendencies. Students are encouraged to join the Communist party and to help the government to enforce its new policies and to carry out propaganda work among the people. Many students join the "South Bound Working Corps" to help in the administration of South China. Others take part in the agrarian reform and educational and cultural work in the rural areas of East China.[10]

Another new feature in the colleges and universities is the prevalence of "study groups", "confabulations", and "lecture clubs", which function with great enthusiasm. Student meetings are often held on the campus and are directed by teachers of political science. The purpose

---

9J. S. Yu, "Education in Communist China," *China Missionary Bulletin*, III (September, 1950), 742.

10"University Graduates' Letter to Mao Tse-tung," *China Missionary Bulletin*, II (August, 1950), 661.

of these meetings is to stimulate progressive ideas among the students. Students of the arts and social sciences are required to go to areas of minority races to make field surveys, so as to learn to handle practical problems in addition to their knowledge aquired from books.[11]

Faculty

The appointment and the removal of teachers in colleges and universities must be approved by the Communist Ministry of Education. In order to assure the national character of the educational program and the inculcation of Communist principles, the chief administrative officers of private institutions must be native Chinese. The responsibility is placed on the shoulders of college professors to see to it that nothing reactionary is approved in the classrooms. They are actually watched by agents to see that this duty is carried out. Sometimes teachers are accused by students of being "reactionary" and the result is that the teachers concerned have to go to the "Reactionary Training School" for reform of their opinions.[12]

At the beginning of each school term, professors must submit their schedules and detailed outlines of teaching

---

[11]Lindsay, op. cit., p.176.
[12]Henry K. Standard, "Private Educational Institutions," China Missionary Bulletin, II (August, 1950), 661.

materials to a small discussion group with Communist party members participating for approval. Very often these outlines are turned down. New outlines must be submitted and approved before classes are permitted to start.[13] Sometimes faculty members have to assume the routine administration of the institution in order to release some of the office personnel for more productive work. The salary scale for an office clerk is too low to warrant the support of a family and dependents. Consequently he has to engage in some form of productive work.[14]

Formerly only professors and persons of high academic status attended faculty meetings. Now such meetings are open to persons of lower status as well. All decisions must be discussed and approved by the Communist party members in the institution before they go into effect.[15] Teachers who taught under the Kuomintang Government must be trained in the light of the new curricula. Apropos of this is the following comment taken from the Communist supported newspaper, Wen Wei Pao, on October 28, 1949:

---

[13] J. S. Yu, *op. cit.*, p.748.

[14] "Some New Educational Developments in China," *China Weekly Review*, CXIV (September, 1949), 115.

[15] *Ibid.*, p.132.

> The people's educational policy aims at revolutionizing the teachers for the benefit of the pupils. Teachers are the executives of an educational policy; they are the guides of the pupils in thoughts, activities, work and learning. In the minds of these formerly employed teachers, many unsound notions still remain, and if their minds were not thoroughly reshaped and adapted to the needs of a new education in the people's democracy, not only would it be impossible for them to maintain their posts by state approval, but they would not even be tolerated by the pupils.[16]

Student Body

Kuo Mo-jo, Vice-Premier of Communist China, claimed recently that in 1953 there were 220,000 students in colleges and universities.[17] However, the general academic standard has taken a marked drop, due to the Communist policy which emphasizes the training of devoted workers rather than scholars. To expel a student is impossible, whatever the cause may be. All must be allowed to stay, even those unqualified for academic work. Poor students are permitted to remain, and must repeat their courses until they pass them.[18]

Students are organized into groups in order to promote interest in reading books and attending meetings. During

---

16 Wen Wei Pao, Hong Kong, October 28, 1949.
17 The Asian Student, October 9, 1953.
18 China Missionary Belletin, II (March, 1950), 258.

the winter and spring vacations, they are required to remain in school for a course of "mind reeducation." The authorities recommend that only a few scholarships be provided for exceptionally bright students. Average students may continue their education by paying full tuition, or are welcome to join the Communist army. Owing to their financial plight, many students are forced to take the latter choice.[19]

Graduates are subject to the control and service of the government. According to the Communist official report in 1950, more than 70,000 youth went to work in government departments, and factories, or joined the army after graduating from schools in East China.[20] Instead of going to Europe and America, many graduates went to the U.S.S.R. and other countries behind the Iron Curtain for advanced studies. The Procommunist Ta Kung Pao of Hongkong (daily newspaper) reported recently that 519 Chinese students went to Russia to study in universities in Moscow, Leningrad, Kiev and Odessa; and 31 students went to Berlin for further study in East German universities in scientific, technical and cultural fields. On the other hand, more than

---

[19] China Missionary Bulletin, II (February, 1950), 180.
[20] China Missionary Bulletin, II (April, 1950), 389.

500 foreign students have studied in Chinese universities on the mainland of China since the Communist took over. They came from East Germany, Czechoslovakia, Poland, Romania, Bulgaria, North Korea, Outer Mongolia and Vietnam. Most of them were exchange students.[21]

Financial Support

All school finances, formerly not subject to public scrutiny, are now made public. All schools are compelled to give regular detailed reports on all expenditures. All the bills are posted in loose leaf notebooks, and every item of them is read in the presence of teachers and representatives of the students. The administration of finances and properties in mission institutions is conducted by native Chinese. The assets of the school can not be used for other purposes than expenses. No change may be made in the legal status of properties of private schools without consent of the Ministry of Education.[22]

In the case of private institutions charging tuition fees, financial accounts must be made public, and committees representing teachers, students, and workers

---

[21] Ta Kung Pao of Hongkong (daily newspaper) October 2, 1953.

[22] Communist Ministry of Education, The Temporary Regulations of the Management of Private Institutions of Higher Learning in August, 1950 (Peiping, China: Ministry of Education, 1950), pp.2-13.

determine tuition charges. Many students in private schools now refuse to pay tuition, claiming that under Communist rule education is free. All these schools depend mainly upon tuitions for their financial support, many of them have to ask the Communist authorities for loans or subsidies to take care of the balance of the budget of the school year. Added to this difficulty is the competition offered by Communist universities set up for the purpose of training political workers quickly and as many as possible. As these universities require only two to four years for graduation, and students are given free room and board and the promise of a job after graduation, some students quit private schools to join the Communist universities. The result is that private institutions are under heavy economic pressure and are declining in enrollment.[23]

Under the Communist regime many private institutions, especially mission schools, have been shut off from their major source of support from abroad, and lack sufficient funds for maintenance or further expansion. As a result they are either closed or taken over by Communist educational authorities. All teacher salaries are calculated

---

[23]<u>China Missionary Bulletin</u>, I (October,1949), 143.

according to class hours, irrespective of experience and years of service. In some cases, young inexperienced teachers get more than their senior colleagues.[24]

B. The Attitude of the Communist Government Toward Private Schools

Under the new regime, education is no longer the property of private organizations or a matter of private enterprise. All private schools are under the strict control of the government though they have a recognized status. Except for the source of financial support, there is no difference at all between private and public schools. Even the finances and budget are subject to government control, and all personnel must be officially approved. Subjects fostering Communist principles such as Marxism, Leninism and Mao Tse-tung's New Democracy are compulsory in all private schools. Every private school must have al least one teacher appointed by the government. These teachers are Communists or government political representatives and usually teach political science. With the pressure toward conformity and uniformity, private education

---

[24]United Board for Christian Colleges in China, Annual Report for the Year 1951 (New York: United Board for Christian Colleges in China, 1951), p.5.

eventually will be thoroughly overhauled and systematically revamped according to the Communist plan.[25]

During the year 1950, the Communist Ministry of Education issued a series of Regulations and Instructions for Institutions of Higher Learning aiming at strengthening the educational authority of the government in regard to both public and private institutions. According to these regulations, private institutions must apply for new registration; permission must be obtained before they are established or discontinued; and the property of the school cannot be treated as private property, and cannot be moved or sold privately at will.[26]

As regards mission schools, Catholic and Protestant, the government requires that they must follow the orders of the government. Foreigners may teach in these schools, but they absolutely cannot give any religious instruction or oblige students to attend religious services and activities. School affairs are conducted by a committee representing teachers, students and workers. The mission

---

[25] "Education in Communist China," World Today, VIII (March, 1950), 264.

[26] Communist Ministry of Education, The Temporary Regulations of Management of Private Institutions of Higher Learning Issued in August, 1950, p.12.

schools are also required to teach Marxist materialism, and to take part in all officially sponsored propaganda campaigns and indoctrination programs.[27] In the summer of 1950, mission schools were told by the educational authorities that they should try to wean themselves from the financial support and nurture of missions abroad. The government promised financial aid in this movement. However, it was generally understood that government subsidies would mean more rigid government control. In fact, there was in many areas a complete disruption of existing school authorities, and a marked tendency to take over mission schools.[28]

C. The Present Status of Private Institutions of Higher Learning

1. Nondenominational Schools

According to a statement of the Chinese Youth Bulletin, October, 1952, in the winter of 1949, when the People's Republic of China was founded, there were 191 universities and colleges and professional schools throughout the country, with a total of over 130,000 students. By 1951, there

---

[27] China Missionary Bulletin, I (November, 1949), 272.

[28] John F. Donovan, "Schools Count in China, The Contribution of the Church and the Attitude of the Communist Government," American Ecclesiastical Review, CXXV (November, 1951), 378-80.

were approximately 200 institutions of higher learning. Of these, 61 percent were public institutions, the remainder private. At the same time the enrollment increased to 219,700 students.[29]

At the beginning of the new regime, the government did not interfere with private individuals and groups continuing their schools, because it did not have the financial means and personnel to provide the needed educational facilities. Besides, nondenominational institutions of higher learning were concentrated for the most part in the urban centers, and the Communists had little experience in dealing with complex educational issues. In many instances, Communist authorities have exercised control by dismissing some of the personnel appointed by the former regime, and by encouraging reorganization for which they themselves provide general political guidance rather than forcing it by harsh or repressive measures.[30]

However, it is usual for a list of partisan workers to be posted in each school under the guise of professional students who practically assume full leadership in all school activities. In Shanghai, a Communist sponsored

---

[29] "Three Years of People's Educatión," Chinese Youth Bulletin, III (October, 1952), 5-6.

[30] Michael Lindsay, op. cit., p.194.

Association of Higher Learning is established for the indoctrination of the professors who were educated in Europe, America or Japan. They are required to attend three months of indoctrination, if they wish to continue to teach.[31]

2. Protestant Schools

In 1949, the doors of Protestant institutions were still open. Many Western faculty members remained at their posts; United Board aid was still welcome; and changes in curriculum were not so drastic as to prove completely unacceptable. But after the outbreak of the war in Korea, the status of Protestant institutions definitely changed. More and more time was to be given to patriotic activities and propaganda campaigns. The task of preserving academic standards and Christian ideals became increasingly difficult. Western faculty members were now accused of imperialistic notions or subversive actions.[32]

Until the end of 1950, Protestant institutions were still in direct contact and receiving help from foreign sponsoring organizations. But on December 30, 1950, the People's Central Government issued an order to freeze the assets of

---

[31] "Communist Training for Youths in China," South China Morning Post, March 29, 1950, 6.

[32] United Board for Christian Colleges in China, Annual Report for the Year of 1951 (New York: United Board for Christian Colleges in China, 1951), pp. 3-4.

foreigners. These institutions thus started the new year shut off from their usual major source of support. Many had insufficient funds to maintain their schools. In the early part of 1951, representatives of all Protestant institutions of higher learning in China met in Peiping where they learned from the Minister of Education that financial aid would come from the government. They were ordered to sever all ties with mission boards abroad especially the United Board in New York. Consequently, all Protestant institutions were taken over by the Communists.[33]

3. Catholic Schools

From the beginning, relations between the new government and the Catholic Church were more hostile than with Protestant groups. The total number of Catholic ecclesiastical divisions on the mainland of China was 143. Twenty nine of the Sees were administered by Chinese bishops. In 1952, after the expulsion of foreign bishops from China, the number of prelates in Red China was reduced to 54. The Communists by means of bribes and threats tried to launch the Independent Church Movement in order to sever relations between the Church and the Holy See. After it was rejected by the firmness and courage of the native

[33]<u>Ibid</u>., p.5.

clergy as well as foreign missionaries, many priests and nuns were imprisoned, or placed under house arrest. Some of them were expelled from the mainland of China and went to Hong Kong.[34]

On October 12, 1950, an official announcement broadcast from Peiping declared that the Communist authorities there had taken over the Catholic University of Peiping. The trouble arose over the insistance by the government of appointing five professors to the staff of the University. Three of them were appointed for the specific purpose of attacking religion in their lectures. The Fathers of the Society of the Divine Word in charge of the school refused to pay the salaries of these hostile teachers. In the meantime, the Congregation of Propaganda, on the recommendation of the Fathers, ceased sending grants from Rome. This cessation of funds irritated the Communists and led them to take control of the University.[35]

In 1951, Aurora University of Shanghai was taken over by the Communists, and became a part of the people's educational enterprise. The University is no longer administered by the French Jesuits, but is under the direct

---

[34]Richard Willier, "Catholic Church in Shanghai," <u>China Missionary Bulletin</u>, IV (November, 1952), 727.

[35]"Communist Authorities Have Taken Over the Catholic University of Fu Jen," <u>Tablet</u>, CXCVI (October, 1950), 356.

control of a school administrative committee, comprising representatives of students, professors and workingmen, who take full responsibility for the entire administration. Discipline is impossible to enforce. The enrollment had declined though the tuition fees have been reduced a fourth under the new regime.[36]

On August 5, 1951, the Hautes Études, which in 1947 had changed its name to Tsinku University, was taken over by the Ministry of Education of the People's Central Government in Tientsin. The students demanded that the Fathers permit and favour the teaching of Marxism, Communism and atheism. The Fathers refused to comply with such a demand. Then the students' committee asked that the Rector, Fr. Alfed Benningus, S.J., resign. All the priests of the University staff resigned with him. They were accused of working for Fascists, of being in league with the U.S. army, and of forming the anti-Communist "Legion of Mary."[37]

Summary

The year 1949 marked the Communist control of the mainland of China and the establishment of the People's Central

---

[36] J. Miral, "A L'Université L'Aurora," China Missionary Bulletin, IV (December, 1952), 797-805.

[37] Hsiao Chien, "A Catholic University Transformed From Serving Imperialism to Serving the People," People's China, No.4, Feb.16, 1952, p.21.

Government at Peiping headed by Mao Tse-tung. As a result, education, public and private, was definitely controlled by the government. The Soviet educational system as well as its methods of teaching were adopted by the Chinese Communists.

Communist education means the teaching of Communist principles and the Communist philosophy of life. All education must be nationalized, popularized, and made scientific. The main task of higher education is to train leaders for national service and reconstruction. Science, engineering, agriculture and medicine are emphasized; while the liberal arts are neglected, and religion prohibited. Private schools are administered by administrative committees, comprising professors, instructors, students and workingmen. The position of dean of discipline in the schools has been abolished.

Courses of study in colleges and universities have been shortened to three years and are largely practical. Political science made up of Communist principles and Marxist economics is dominant. Students are encouraged to study the teachings of Marx, Lenin, Stalin and Mao Tse-tung. Russian textbooks have been translated into Chinese for school use. Teaching is based on discussion, and favors small groups. Students who disagree with the teachers are classified as reactionaries, and are sent to the "Big Class" and "Discussion Groups" for further indoctrination.

In each school there is an official youth organization, New Democracy Youth Fellowship, for the purpose of promoting party programs. Study groups, confabulations and lecture clubs are an essential part of school organization. Students are encouraged to join the Communist party and to participate in agrarian reform and propaganda in rural areas. However, the academic standards of the schools are low. Graduates are required to put themselves at the service of the government. Some graduates of colleges and universities have gone to the U.S.S.R. and other countries behind the Iron Curtain for advanced studies.

The appointment and dismissal of a teacher in private schools must be approved by the Communist Ministry of Education. Former teachers must attend the "Revolutionary Training School" for re-education before they may continue to teach. Professors must submit the outlines of courses to a select group together with Communist party members for approval. Teachers salaries are culculated according to class hours, irrespective of experience and years of service. All school finances must be made public.

According to the regulations promulgated by the Ministry of Education, private institutions must apply for new registration; permission must be obtained before they are established or discontinued; and the assets of the school cannot be used for purposes other than school expenses. Mission schools are prohibited to give religious instruction or to oblige students to attend religious services and activities.

At present, private individuals and groups are permitted to continue their schools, because the government does not have the financial means not the personnel to provide adequate educational facilities. However, Communist authorities exercise control over them indirectly by dismissing some of the personnel in nondenominational schools, and by encouraging reorganization of these institutions with Communist political guidance. A number of partisan workers are assigned to each school as so-called professional students in order to assume leadership in all school activities.

At first the status of Protestant institutions of higher learning remained the same. After the outbreak of the war in Korea, these schools met with political interference and economic pressure. The task of preserving academic standards and Christian ideals became increasingly difficult. In 1950, the government issued an order to freeze the assets of foreigners in China. Consequently, these institutions were shut off from their major source of support. In 1951, all Protestant institutions were taken over by the Communists.

The Catholic Church has suffered greatly under the new regime. In 1952, the number of bishops in Red China was reduced from 143 to 54. The Communists launched the Independent Church Movement with the hope of separating the Church from Rome. Many priests and nuns gave their lives for their religious beliefs; others were put in prison or placed under house arrest. Others were expelled from the mainland of China and went to Hong Kong. On October 12, 1950, the Catholic University of Peiping was taken over by the government, because the Fathers of the Society of the Divine Word refused to accept five professors appointed by the government to the staff of the University. In 1951, both Aurora University of Shanghai and Tsinku University of Tientsin, conducted by the French Jesuits were taken over by the Communist authorities. The former was placed under the direct control of a school committee approved by the government. The latter was reorganized, because the Fathers rejected the students' demand to permit the teaching of Marxism, Communism and atheism in the school. All the priests of the administration and teaching staff resigned.

Chapter VI

Summary and Conclusions

The problem involved in this study has been to trace in chronological order the growth and development of privately controlled institutions of higher learning in China from the time of the Republic in 1912 to the present. There were approximately seventy-nine schools, eighteen of which were established before the Republic. These schools may be conveniently divided into nondenominational, Protestant, and Catholic institutions of higher learning. Important phases of their history, such as organization and administration, faculty, curriculum, finance, student body, buildings and equipment have been treated. However, the study has not attempted, because of inadequate information, to deal with those private schools that have not been registered or recognized by the Ministry of Education.

From 1912 to 1936, fifty of the one hundred and eight institutions of higher learning in China were established by private enterprise. Of these thirty-two were nondenominational, sixteen were Protestant, and three were Catholic schools. Nine were founded in North China, twenty-three in East China, ten in Central China, seven in South

China, and one in Northwest China. Forty-eight institutions were coeducational, and two were for girls exclusively. Twenty-three were universities, nineteen were independent colleges, and eight were professional schools. The number of institutions of each of these categories varied, however, from year to year until 1929, when the Ministry of Education of the Nationalist Government issued basic laws governing higher education.

The nondenominational institutions of higher learning were established mostly by private individuals, philanthropic and social organizations. Fuh Tan University was the first institution established by Chinese private enterprise in 1904. Amoy University was the first private institution of higher learning registered with the Ministry of Education in 1920. Two institutions, Nankai University and Chaoyang College, offered graduate work and conferred the Master of Arts degree; while the others awarded only the Bachelor degree in arts and sciences. Between 1926 and 1927, due to political unrest, some institutions such as Chunghua University of Wuchang, Shanghai College of Law and Political Science, Shanghai School of Fine Arts, and Wuchang School of Fine Arts were temporarily discontinued.

Of sixteen Protestant institutions of higher learning, eight were union schools supported by several denominational missions, and six were denominational. Two institutions, Lingnan University and Hsiang Ya Medical College, were strictly nonsectarian, though they were begun and partly supported by the Protestant missions. All were coeducational except Ginling and Hua Nan which were colleges exclusively for women. With the exception of St. John's University, these schools were registered with the Ministry of Education. Most of these institutions had obtained charters from the states of New York, Tennessee, Virginia, Connecticut; and from Washington, D.C. and Canada. They were supported by thirty-eight different missions and by the United Boards of America, Britain and Canada.

The educational work of the Catholic Church in China extended over the whole country and included every level, from the elementary school to the university. By 1935, the total number of schools which the Church maintained throughout China was 14,446; and the total number of pupils was 378,248. However, Catholic educators emphasized educational work among the masses which was largely religious instruction. In the field of higher education, there were only three institutions. Aurora University, founded in 1903, was under the direction of the French Jesuits. Among the three colleges of medicine, law, engineering and science, the school of medicine had the largest enrollment. The Heude Museum of Natural History, which was connected with it, was one of the finest of its kind in the East. The Tientsin College of Industry and Commerce, founded in 1923 by the Jesuits of the Province of Champagne, France, specialized in industry and commerce. Among the best known schools of higher learning was the Catholic University of Peiping, which was founded in 1925 by the Holy See, and entrusted to the American Cassinese Congregation of Benedictines. In 1933, it was given over to the care of the Society of the Divine Word. This University, which comprised a striking group of buildings in Chinese style, gained a high reputation for its courses in literature and science; while its school of art spread the knowledge and ideals of Christian culture throughout the nation. In addition, Ricci Hall of Hong Kong was founded in 1929 by the Irish Jesuits for the accommodation and instruction of students attending Hong Kong University.

During the period of the Sino-Japanese War (1937-1945),

the development of higher education in China was greatly affected. Many institutions were destroyed or damaged by the Japanese. Some were forced to move to the interior where they combined with others to form "Federated Universities" or "Associated Colleges." The cultural centers of China shifted from the North and the East Coast to cities of western provinces, such as Kunming, Kweiyang, Chungking, Kweilin, and Chengtu. These refugee institutions suffered from lack of adequate facilities and books. They carried on their work by receiving aid from the government and abroad. The universities of Nankai, Amoy, and Hsiang Ya Medical College became national institutions with financial support from the government. However, a number of private institutions still remained in the occupied areas, such as Peiping and Shanghai.

Despite the war, the number of institutions of higher learning apparently increased. From 1937 to 1948, thirty-four new private institutions of higher learning were established. Of these thirty-two were nondenominational schools, and two were Catholic colleges for women. Four were universities, fourteen were colleges, and sixteen were professional schools. By 1948, according to the Ministry of Education, there were 207 universities, colleges, and professional schools, of which 79 were private schools.

During the war, most of the Protestant institutions of higher learning were moved to Szechwan, Yunnan, Kwangsi and Fukien provinces. The schools of Nanking, Yenching, Soochow, Cheeloo, and Ginling College for Women joined the West China Union University in Chengtu, and these became the Associated Universities. In Shanghai, the schools of Shanghai, St. John's, Soochow, and Hangchow Christian College worked together and formed the Associated Christian Colleges. Between 1945 and 1946, these institutions returned to their former campuses and enjoyed their prewar status.

All Catholic institutions of higher learning remained on their own campuses and continued their work during the war. Aurora University under the direction of the Jesuits of the Province of Paris, France, in the French Concession of Shanghai did an exceptional service for the nation in keeping learning alive. Tientsin College of Industry and Commerce, known also as Hautes Etudes, was expanded and raised to the status of a university in 1947, and changed its name to Tsinku University. The Catholic University of Peiping remained in Peiping. The Ecclesiastical Institute for Chinese priests, a graduate school of arts and sciences, and a museum for oriental ethnology were added to the University during the war. Two Catholic colleges for women - Aurora College for Women and the Women's College of the Catholic University of Peiping - were founded in 1938. The former was under the direction of the Sisters of the Society of the Sacred Heart; and the latter was entrusted to the Sisters Servants of the Holy Ghost.

Under the Nationalist regime, higher education was conducted in three kinds of institutions - the university, the independent college, and the professional school. According to the educational laws, a university should at least consist of three colleges; otherwise, it was known as an independent college, which might have two faculties. The universities were divided into colleges according to certain subjects or groups of subjects, such as the liberal arts, sciences, law, commerce, agriculture, medicine, engineering and education. These colleges were divided for purposes of organization and teaching into departments. There were universities with five, six or seven colleges; some had only three in order to be recognized by the State. Both university and college courses were four years, except in the case of medicine which required six years. The professional school trained students in some special branch of applied science or the fine arts, the period of training being one or two years less than that of the university or independent college.

As for internal organization, schools were organized in accordance with the regulations and requirements issued by the Ministry of Education. Eash school was governed by a board of trustees, which had the power to establish the general policy, to manage the finances, and to appoint the president of the school. Under the president were offices of studies, discipline, and business management, each with a certain number of divisions and a respective dean. In addition, there were special committees dealing with entrance examinations, scholarship funds, library, publications, and buildings; all of these varied from school to school.

The program of studies was also outlined by the Ministry of Education with minor differences. The extracurricular activities varied in the different schools. Among them were student government, clubs, and athletic teams. The academic year consisted of two semesters, from September 1st to the latter part of January, and from February tenth to the end of June. The sources of annual income likewise varied in the schools. However, most funds were derived from student fees, private donations, invested endowment and government subsidies.

In 1949, the Communists completely controlled the mainland of China; and the People's Central Government was established at Peiping. Under the new regime, both public and private schools came under the strict control of the government. The main objective of higher education was to train leaders for national service and reconstruction. Schools were administered by administrative committees, comprising professors, instructors, students, and workers. Science and practical studies were emphasized; while the liberal arts were neglected and religion prohibited. Cources for colleges and universities were shortened to three years. Students were required to study the teaching of Marx, Lenin, Stalin, and Mao Tse-tung. The method of education aimed to unify theory and practice. Instruction was based on discussion, and given in small groups. Graduates of colleges and universities were subject to the control and service of the government. The appointment and dismissal of teachers in private institutions had to be approved by the educational authorities.

At first the Communist authorities exercised indirect control of nondenominational schools by dismissing the

the personnel appointed by the former regime, and by encouraging reorganization with Communist political guidance. However, with the tendency toward conformity and uniformity, these institutions eventually will be thoroughly overhauled, and brought into line with the Communist plan. Mission schools, Catholic and Protestant, are required to teach Marxist materialism, and to take part in all officially sponsored propaganda campaigns and indoctrination programs. All school finances are made public and the assets of the school cannot be treated as private property or sold at will. Religious instruction is prohibited, and students may not be required to attend religious services or activities. By 1951, all mission schools were taken over by the Communists. At that time, there were approximately in China, 200 institutions of higher learning with a total enrollment of 219,700 students. Of these, sixty-one percent were public institutions, and the other thirty-nine percent private.

Private higher education has played an important role in China. It made a remarkable contribution to Chinese educational development. Under the Kuomintang government over forty percent of all institutions of higher learning in the country were established by private enterprise.

Nearly fifty percent of the students in colleges and universities were registered in private schools. The philanthropic interest displayed by the supporters of these schools was remarkable. Private institutions offered an academic freedom which was not possible in government schools. They enlisted the support of the communities; and won the professional enthusiasm and devotion of the teaching staff and administrative officers in a way that was most significant. Hundreds of students were graduated from these institutions; and they held important positions in society as well as in offices of government.

Through the pioneer work of the mission schools, modern education and Western learning were introduced into China. Christian education enjoyed a gratifying measure of public confidence. Not only were the mission schools well-equipped but they were also particularly successful in the formation of character by means of religious instruction. The unselfishness and sacrifice of the missionaries were perhaps the most important factors in their success.

Higher education in China now faces a crisis. Academic standards, the promotion of research, and the geographical distribution of the schools have been perplexing problems. The present movement to make education practical, vocational and scientific is accompanied by the dissemination of a naturalistic philosophy. This materialistic viewpoint has helped to advance the cause of Communist throughout the country. It is true that China needs more and more engineers, chemists and all sorts of technicans in order to transform this country which is backward agriculturally into an industrialized state. However, the advantages of science alone can not help China to build itself into a prosperous and peaceful nation. What China needs is Christian education which seeks the highest values of life and helps to form the "perfect man", the Christlike man. Chinese Christian leaders and gentlemen must be developed in whose souls is the life of Christ, gentlemen who are educated not only for time, but for eternity.

Bibliography

Primary Sources (Chinese)

Government Publications (annual government reports, educational laws, proceedings, bulletins, and statistics)

Chiao-yu-pu (Ministry of Education). Chiao-yu Fa-ling Hui-pien (Educational Laws and Ordinances). Chungking, China: Ministry of Education, 1942. Pp.586.

________. Chiao-yu Fa-ling Hsu-pien (Educational Laws and Ordinances, Supplement). Nanking, China: Ministry of Education, 1945. Pp.112.

________. Chiao-yu-pu Kung-pao (Ministry of Education Gazette). Nanking, China: Ministry of Education, 1929-48. Weekly.

________. Chiao-yu-pu Shih-cha-ko-shen-shih Chiao-yu Hui-pien (A General Report of the Educational Inspection of the Provinces and Special Cities in China). Nanking, China: Ministry of Education, 1933. Pp.347.

________. Chiao-yu-pu Shu-chin Shih-li Hsueh-hsia Fa-ling (Revised Regulations for Private Schools). Nanking, China: Ministry of Education, 1933. Pp.34.

________. Chiao-yu-pu Tu-hsueh Shih-cha Hupeh Kiangsi Erh-sheng Chiao-yu Pao-kao (The Report of the Educational Inspectors of the Ministry of Education in the Provinces of Hupeh and Kiangsi). Nanking, China: Ministry of Education, 1933. Pp.195.

________. Chiao-yu-pu Wen-tu Hui-pien (A Collection of Important Documents of Education). Nanking, China: Ministry of Education, 1942. Pp.478.

________. Chung-hua Min-kuo Chiao-yu Tung-chi (Statistics On Education, 1941). Chungking, China: Ministry of Education, 1942. Pp.98.

________. Chung-hua Min-kuo Erh-shih-su-nien-tu Chuan Kao Chiao-yu Tung-chi Chien-pien (Country-wide Statistical Abstract On Education For the Year, 1935). Shanghai, China: The Commercial Press, Ltd., 1938. Pp.78.

__________. Chung-hua Min-kuo Kao-teng Chiao Tung-chi (Country-wide Statistics On Higher Education, 1928-35). Nanking, China: Ministry of Education, 1936. Pp.206.

__________. Chung-kuo Chiao-yu Hui-i Pao-kao (Proceedings of the National Educational Conference). Nanking, China: Ministry of Education, 1928. Pp.1024.

__________. Chung-kuo Chuan-kuo I-shan Hsueh-hsia Yao-lang Summary Review of the Institutions of Higher Learning in China). Shanghai, China: Ching-chung Book Co., 1942. Pp.377.

__________. Ta-hsueh Ko-moo Pao (List of University Courses). Chungking, China: Ministry of Education,1940. Pp.135.

__________. Ti-erh-tsu Chung-kuo Chiao-yu Nien-chien (The Second China Educational Yearbook). Shanghai, China: The Commercial Press, Ltd., 1948.Pp.1643.

__________. Ti-I-tsu Chung-kuo Chiao-yu Nien-chien (The First China Educational Yearbook). Shanghai, China: Kai-ming Book Co., 1934. Pp.1153.

Honan Chiao-yu-ting (Bureau of Education of Honan Province). Honan-shan Chiao-yu Tung-chi (The Educational Statistics of Honan Province). Changsha, China: Bureau of Education of Honan Province, 1931. Pp.136.

Huang, Yen-pei. Huang Yen-pei Kao-cha Chiao-yu Ni-chi (Huang Yen-pei's Diary During His Investigation of the State of Education). Shanghai, China: The Commercial Press, Ltd., 1915. 2 vols.

Kiangsi Chiao-yu-ting (Bureau of Education of Kiangsi Province). Kiangsi-shan Chiao-yu Pao-kao (Annual Educational Report of the Province of Kiangsi). Nanchang, Kiangsi, China: Bureau of Education of Kiangsi Province, 1947. Pp.187.

Kwangtung Chiao-yu-ting (Bureau of Education of Kwangtung Province). Chiang-ho Hua-nan Chiao-yu (The Report of Postwar Education in South China). Canton, China: Bureau of Education of Kwangtung Province, 1947. Pp.165.

Lin-min-chi-fu (People's Central Government). Chien-wu-hui-i Kwang-yu Hsueh-chi Kai-kuo-ti Kiu-ting (The Cultural and Educational Policy Adopted by the Chinese People's Consultative Conference in 1949). Peiping, China: Ministry of Education, 1950. Pp.104.

__________. Lin-min Shu-cha (People's Handbook). Peiping, China: Department of State, 1952. Pp.749.

__________. Shu-li Hsueh-hsia Kwang-li Chan-hen Tai-li (The Temporary Regulations for the Management of Private Institutions of Higher Learning). Peiping, China: Ministry of Education, 1950. Pp.34.

Shanghai Chiao-yu-ku (Board of Education of Shanghai). Shanghai Chiao-yu Tung-chi (Statistics On Education in Shanghai). Shanghai, China: Board of Education of Shanghai, 1929. Pp.237.

Shu, Hsin-cheng. Chin-tai Chung-kuo Chiao-yu Shu-liao (Historical Materials On Modern Education in China). Shanghai, China: Chunghua Book Co., 1923. 4 vols.

Shu, Yuan-chin. Shanghai Ta-tung-shaw Hsueh-hsia Tao-cha-lu (Directory of Shanghai Schools, Elementary, Secondary and Higher). Shanghai, China: Lung-wen Book Co., 1935. Pp.211.

Szechwan Chiao-yu-ting (Bureau of Education of Szechwan Province). Szechwan-shan Chiao-yu Pao-kao (Annual Report of the Bureau of Education of the Provincial Government of Szechwan). Chengtu, Szechwan, China: Bureau of Education of Szechwan Province, 1948. Pp.254.

Annual School Reports, Catalogues, Yearbooks

Chengmin Hsueh-yuan Shih-chou-nien Hsueh-kien (The Tenth Anniversary of Chengmin College of Arts). Shanghai, China: Chengmin College of Arts Press, 1938. Pp.153.

Chishing Non-yei Chuan-ko Hsueh-hsia Nien-kien (The Yearbook of Chishing School of Agriculture, 1947). Tao-tu, Shensi. China: Chishing School of Agriculture Press, 1947. Pp.76.

Chiuching Shan-yei Chuan-ko Hsueh-hsia Chien-jung (Catalogue of Chiuching School of Commerce, 1945-46).

Chuhai Ta-hsueh Nien-kien (The Yearbook of Chuhai University, 1947). Canton, China: Chuhai University Press, 1947. Pp.138.

Chungfa Ta-hsueh Chien-jung (Catalogue of Franco-Chinese University, 1936-37).

Chunghua Kung-shan Chuan-ko Hsueh-hsia Nien-kien (The Yearbook of Chunghua School of Engineering and Commerce, 1947). Shanghai, China: Chunghua

School of Engineering and Commerce Press, 1947. Pp.145.

Chunghua Wen-fa Hsueh-yuan Chien-jung (Catalogue of Chunghua College of Arts And Law, 1947-48).

Chunghui Shan-yei Chuan-ko Hsueh-hsia Chien-jung (Catalogue of Chunghui School of Commerce, 1947-48).

Chungkuo Hsueh-yuan Shih-liu-chou-nien Hsueh-kien (The Sixteen Anniversary of the China College of Peiping). Peiping, China: China College Press, 1927. Pp.135.

Fuchen Fa-hsueh-yuan Chien-jung (Catalogue of Fuchen College of Law, 1947-48).

Fukien Hsueh-yuan Sun-shih-chou-nien Hsueh-kien (The Thirtieth Anniversary of Fukien College, 1940). Foochow, Fukien, China: Fukien College Press, 1940. Pp.232.

Hanhua Non-yei Chuan-ko Hsueh-hsia Nien-kien (The Yearbook of Hanhua School of Agriculture, 1947). Chungking, China: Hanhua School of Agriculture Press, 1947. Pp.136.

Huakao Kung-shan Hsueh-yuan Chien-jung (Catalogue of the Overseas Chinese College of Engineering and Commerce, 1947-48).

Kiangnan Ta-hsueh Nien-kien (The Yearbook of Kiangnan University, 1948). Wusih, Kiangsu, China: Kiangnan University Press, 1948. Pp.253.

Kwangchow Ta-hsueh Shih-kiu-chou-nien Hsueh-kien (The Ninteenth Anniversary of the University of Canton, 1946). Canton, China: University of Canton Press, 1946. Pp.214.

Kwanghua Ta-hsueh Shih-chou-nien Hsueh-kien (The Tenth Anniversary of Kwanghua University, 1935). Shanghai, China: Kwanghua University Press, 1935. Pp.186.

Kwanghua Yi-hsueh-yuan Sun-shih-chou-nien Hsueh-kien (The Thirtieth Anniversary of Kwanghua Medical College, 1939). Canton, China: Kwanghua Medical College Press, 1939. Pp.109.

Lisin Kiu-kee Chuan-ko Hsueh-hsia Chien-jung (Catalogue of Lisin Accounting School, 1936-37).

Minkuo Hsueh-yuan Chien-jung (Catalogue of Minkuo College, 1934-35).

Nankai Ta-hsueh Chien-jung (Catalogue of Nankai University, 1928-29).

Shanghai Fa-hsueh-yuan Chien-jung (Catalogue of Shanghai College of Law, 1933-34).

Shang Huei Wen-fa-hsueh-yuan Chien-jung (Catalogue of Shang Huei College of Arts and Law, 1947-48).

Sinan Mei-shu Chuan-ko Nien-kien (Annual Report of Southwest School of Fine Arts, 1937). Chengtu, China: Southwest School of Fine Arts Press, 1937. Pp.48.

Sin-chung-kuo Fa-shan Hsueh-yuan Chien-jung (Catalogue of New China College of Law and Commerce, 1947-48).

Tung A Ti-yu Chuan-ko Hsueh-hsia Chien-jung (Catalogue of Eastern Asia School of Physical Education, 1933-34).

Tungnan Yi-hsueh-yuan Chien-jung (Catalogue of Tungnan Medical College, 1933-34).

Tungteh Yi-hsueh-yuan Erh-shih-chou-nien Hsueh-kien (The Twentieth Anniversary of the Tungteh Medical College,1938). Shanghai, China: Tungteh Medical College Press, 1938. Pp.208.

Wusih Kuo-hsueh Chuan-shu Hsueh-hsia Nien-kien (Annual Report of Wusih School of Chinese Classics, 1935). Wusih, Kiangsu, China: Wusih School of Chinese Classics Press, 1935. Pp.24.

School Bulletins, Journals, Newspapers

Chaoyang Hsueh-pao (Chaoyang College Bulletin), VII (April, 1947).

Chien Kuo Hsueh-pao (Chien Kuo College Bulletin), III (March, 1946).

Chih Kiang Hsueh-pao (Chih Kiang Bulletin, LXX (January, 1935).

Chunghua Chiao-yu Kai-chin-she Nien-kien (Annual Bulletin of the Chinese National Association for the Advancement of Education), 1923-44. Chinese National Association for the Advancement of Education, Peiping, China.

Fukien Hsueh-pao (Fukien College Bulletin), III (June,1935).

Huakao Ni-pao (China Daily News), July 20, 1953. China Daily News Inc., New York City.

Kuo Min Ta-hsueh Hsia-kien (Kuo Min University Journal), II (1926).

Lingnan Ta-hsueh Hsia-kien (Bulletin of Lingnan University), 1932-1937.

Ming Hsien Hsueh-yuan Yao-kien (Ming Hsien College Monthly), III (June, 1935).

Minkuo Hsueh-kien (Minkuo College Bulletin), V (April, 1924).

Nanfang Ni-pao (South China Morning Post), March 29, 1950.

Nanhua Hsueh-pao (Nanhua College Bulletin), I (1947).
Nantung Hsueh-yuan Yao-kien (Nantung College Monthly), II (July, 1947).
Sinan Shan-yei Chuan-ko Hsueh-hsia-kien (Southwest School of Commerce Bulletin), II (Spring, 1948).
Tahsia Ta-hsueh Hsia-kien (Tahsia University Bulletin), 1923-1931.
Ta Kung Pao (Utopia Daily News), Hongkong, October 28, 1949.
Tsang Lang Mei (Bulletin Of Soochow School of Fine Arts), II (January, 1937).
Tungnan Yi-hsueh-yuan Tao-kien (Tungnan Medical College Journal), VII (June, 1933).
Wen Hua Tu-shu Chuan-ko Hsueh-hsia Che-kien (Wen Hua or Boone Library School Quarterly), 1929-31.

Primary Sources (Western languages)

Annuaire des missions Catholigues en Chine, 1933-36. Bureau Sinologigue de Zikaiwei, Shanghai, China.
Annual of Catholic Missions in China. Peiping, China: Imprimerie des Lazaristes, 1935.
Bauer, Thomas J. The Systematic Destruction of the Catholic Church in China. Published in the series "World Horizon Reports," New York, N.Y., 1954. This document charges that between the years 1950 and 1954 the Communist Government of China systematically maneuvered the destruction of the Catholic Church in China.
Bulletin de l'Universite l'Aurora, I-XVIII (1921-38).
Bulletin of the Catholic University of Peking, I-VI (1926-29).
Catalogue of Aurora College for Women, 1940-41.
Catalogue of the Catholic University of Peiping, 1936-37; 1947-48.
Catalogue of Fukien Christian Union University, 1935-36.
Catalogue of Hua Nan College for Women, 1934-35.
Catalogue of the University of Shanghai, 1936-37.
Catalogue of Yenching University, 1942-43.
Chang, Chih-tung. China's Only Hope. New York: Fleming H. Revell Co., 1900. Pp.151.
China Centenary Missionary Conference Records; Report of the Great Conference held at Shanghai, April 5th to May 8th, 1907. New York: American Tract Society, 1907. Pp.xxvii-823.

China Christian Education Association. Christian Education in China. New York: Committee and Council of Foreign Missions Conference of North America, 1922. Pp.430.

——————. Conference of Christian Colleges and Universities in China; Report 1924. China Christian Education Association, Bulletin No.3, Shanghai, China.

——————. Conference of Christian Colleges and Universities in China; Second Biennial Report 1926. China Christian Education Association, Bulletin No.16. Shanghai, China.

——————. Faculty Directory. Christian Colleges and Professional Schools of China, 1928-29. China Christian Education Association, Bulletin No.25, Shanghai, China.

——————. Handbook of Christian Colleges and Universities in China. China Christian Education Association, No.14. Shanghai, China, 1926.

——————. Statistical Report of Christian Colleges and Universities in China; 1924-25; 1930-31; 1932-33. China Christian Education Association, Bulletin Nos.8, 28, 30. Shanghai, China.

China Christian Yearbook, 1922-23. Shanghai, China: Christian Literature Society, 1923.

China Educational Commission. The Report of the China Educational Commission of 1921-22. Shanghai, China: The Commercial Press, Ltd., 1922. Pp. iii-390.

China Yearbook, 1916. London: G. Routledge & Sons Ltd., 1916. Pp.xv-799.

China Yearbook, 1924-25. Tientsin, China: The Tientsin Press, Ltd., 1925. Pp.xxxiii-1250.

China Yearbook, 1936-37; 1938-39. Shanghai, China: The North China Daily News and Herald.

Chinese Yearbook, 1935-36. Shanghai, China: The Chinese Yearbook Publishing Co., 1936. Pp.1966.

Chinese Yearbook, 1938-39. Shanghai, China: The Commercial Press, Ltd., 1939. Pp.754.

Chyne, Wen-ya. Handbook of Cultural Institutions in China. Shanghai, China: Chinese National Committee on Intellectual Cooperation, 1936. Pp.282.

Conference on Christian Education in China. Chinese Christian Education; a report of a conference held in New York, April 6th, 1925, under the joint auspices of the International Missionary Council and the Foreign Missions Conference of North China, New York, 1925. Pp.103.

Crow, Carl. Handbook for China. New York: Dodd & Mead Co., 1926. Pp.390.

Educational Directory and Yearbook of China, 1920. Shanghai, China: Edward Evans and Sons, Ltd., 1920. Pp.xlvi-160.

Educational Directory of China. Shanghai, China: The Educational Directory of China Publishing Co., 1920.

Educational Yearbook, 1924, 1929, 1932, 1933, 1938. New York: International Institute of Teachers College of Columbia University.

Institute of International Education. Record of the Testimonial Dinner to Dr. Charles K. Edmunds. New York: Institute of International Education, 1922. Pp.22.

International Institute of Intellectual Cooperation of League of Nations. The Reorganization of Education in China. Paris: League of Nations' Institute of Intellectual Cooperation, 1932. Pp.200.

Laymen's Foreign Missions Inquiry. Regional Report of the Commission of Christian Higher Education. New York: Laymen's Foreign Mission, 1930. Pp.xv-349.

Lindsay, Michael. Notes on Educational Problems in Communist China, 1941-47. New York: International Secretariat, Institute of Pacific Relations, 1950. Pp.194.

MacGillivaray D. (ed.) The China Mission Yearbook, 1941. Shanghai, China: Christian Literature Society for China, 1941.

Ministry of Information. China After Five Years of War New York: Chinese News Service, 1942. Pp.iv-233.

————————. China Handbook, 1937-43. New York: Macmillan Co., 1944. Pp.xvi-862.

————————. China Handbook, 1950. New York: Rockport Press, 1950. Pp.xv-799.

Monroe, Paul. A Report On Education in China. New York: Institute of International Education, 1922. Pp.41.

Rawlinson, Frank. The China Christian Yearbook ,1936-37. Glendale, California: Authur H. Clark Co., 1937.

St. John's University, 1879-1929. Shanghai, China: Kelly and Walsh, Ltd., 1929. Pp.v-92.

Twenty-fifth Anniversary of Soochow University. Soochow, China: Soochow University Press, 1925. Pp.258.

West China Union University Bulletin, I-III (1941-44). Chengtu, China: West China Union University Press.

Yearbook of the Catholic University of Peiping, 1948. Peiping, China: Catholic University of Peiping, 1948. Pp.38.

Secondary Sources (Chinese)

Chang, Chih-chi. Chung Shang Hsien-shen Chih Chiao-yu Su-hsiang (The Educational Theory of Dr. Sun Yat-sen). Shanghai, China: The Commercial Press, Ltd., 1937. Pp.56.

——————. Tsung Tsai Ti Chiao-yu Su-hsiang (The Educational Thought of Generalissimo Chiang Kai-shek). Shanghai, China: The Commercial Press, Ltd., 1939. Pp.78.

Chen, Kao-fu. Chung-kuo Chiao-yu Kai-kao-ti-tu-chien (The Reorganization of Chinese Education). Shanghai, China: Ching-chung Book Co., 1944. Pp.203.

Chen, Chin-che. Chung-kuo Chiao-yu-shu (The History of Chinese Education). Shanghai, China: The Commercial Press, Ltd., 1936. Pp.346.

Chiang, Shu-ko. Chung-kuo Chin-tai Chiao-yu Chih-tu (Modern Educational System of China). Shanghai, China: The Commercial Press, Ltd., 1933. Pp.248.

Chu, Chou-tung. Chung-kuo Hsueh-hsia Chih-tu (The School System of China). Shanghai, China: The Commercial Press, Ltd., 1934. Pp.246.

Chu, Tse-shuang. Chung-kuo Kuo-min-tang Chiao-yu Cheng-tze.(The Educational Policy of Kuomintang). Shanghai, China: The Commercial Press, Ltd., 1938. Pp.267.

Fang, Hao. Chung-kuo Tien-chu-chiao Shih-lung-tsung (History of the Catholic Church in China). Shanghai, China: Chung-ching Book Co., 1939. Pp.238.

Fei, Hsiao-tung. Ta-hsueh-ti Kai-chou (The Reorganization of the University). Shanghai, China: Shanghai Publishing Co., 1950. Pp.132.

Hsiao, Jo-she. Tien-chu-chiao Chuan-hsen Chung-kuo-kao (History of the Catholic Missions in China). Shangtung, China: Catholic Mission, 1937. Pp.460.

Hsiang, C.Y. Ta-hsueh Yu Chung-kuo Min-chu Wen-hua (Higher Education and Chinese National Culture). Shanghai, China: Ching-chung Book Co., 1943. Pp.143.

Kuo, Ping-wen. Chung-kuo Chiao-yu Chih-tu-shu (History of the Chinese Educational System). Shanghai, China: The Commercial Press, Ltd., 1920. Pp.209.

Shin-chin-pao. Peiping Kuo-ta-hsueh-ti Chuan-kan (Universities in Peiping). Peiping, China: New Morning Post, Inc., 1929. Pp.148.

Shu, Hsin-cheng. Chunghua Min-kuo Chih Chiao-yu (Education in the Chinese Republic). Shanghai, China: Chunghua Book Co., 1933. Pp.93.

----------. Chung-kuo Hsin Chiao-yu Kai-kan (New Education in China). Shanghai, China: Chunghua Book Co., 1930. Pp.554.

Tan Yeh et al. Chiao-yu Ta-tzu-shu (Educational Encyclopedia). Shanghai, China: The Commercial Press, Ltd., 1933. Pp.1692.

Tao, Hsin-chi. Chung-kuo Chiao-yu Kai-chin (The Reconstruction of Chinese Education). Shanghai, China: Tung A Library, 1928. Pp.321.

Ting, Chi-pien. Chung-kuo Chin-chi-shih-nien-lai Chiao-yu Chi-shih (Events in Chinese Education During the Last Seventy Years). Shanghai, China: National Institute of Compilation and Trsnslation, 1935. Pp.291.

Yen, Kwei-lai. Hung-chi-hsia-ti Ta-hsueh Chen-huo (Student Life Under Communist Control). Hongkong: Hsin-hua Book Co., 1951. Pp.238.

Periodical Articles (Chinese)

Chang, Chung-kiang. "The Educational Work and Future Plan of the University of Shanghai," Huta Education, I (June, 1933), 72-74.

Chang, Tso-chi. "On the Problem of Mission Schools," Chunghua Educational Review, XIV (February, 1925), 8-12.

Chang, Yin-shu. "New Colleges in Occupied Areas," Educational Bulletin, IV (March, 1942), 32-38.

Chen, Che. "Postwar Education in Kiangsu," Chunghua Educational Review, XXXIX (June, 1948), 50-56.

Chou, Chien-ho. "New Colleges in Szechwan," Educational Bulletin, III (June, 1947), 42-45.

Chou, Tai-yuan. "The Expansion of Chinese Higher Education," Chunghua Educational Review, XII (November, 1923), 1-10.

Chuan, Chi-shun. "Chinese Higher Education," Chunghua Educational Review, XVII (February, 1928), 23-25.

Chu, Ching-nung. "The Position of Christian Schools in the Chinese System of Education," New Education, IV (March, 1922), 355-361.

"College of Science of Cheeloo University," Cheeloo University Bulletin, XXXIII (May, 1943), 8-11.

Hua, Lim-I. "Selective Courses System in Chinese Universities," Chunghua Educational Review, XVII (October, 1925), 32-36.

Kuo, Ping-wen. "Higher Education in 1921," New Education, IV (February, 1922), 225-28.

----------. "Higher Education in 1922," New Education, V (February, 1923), 257-60.

Li, Yu-chuan. "Wartime Education in Shanghai," Chunghua Educational Review, XXI (June, 1947), 34-38.

Lim, Shu-sen. "Art Education in China," Art Monthly, VII (July, 1932), 22-24.

Shu, Hsia-chai. "Higher Education for Women in China," Magazine for Women, XIV (May, 1928), 11-15.

Shu, Ming. "Higher Education in Canton," Chunghua Education Review, XXXIX (March, 1948), 43-47.

Tung, Shen. "Chengfu School of Textile Engineering in Shanghai," Educational Bulletin, IV (Sept., 1948), 33-38.

Wang, Shi-ting. "Plan for the Reorganization of Shanghai Higher Education," New Educational Review, III (April, 1927), 3-6.

Yen, Li-hsien. "The Events in the Last Fifteen Years in the Development of Soochow School of Fine Arts," Tsang Lang Mei, II (February, 1937), 32-38.

Secondary Sources (Western languages)

Books

Abel, James F. A Survey of Education in Countries Other Than the United States. U.S. Office of Education, Bulletin 37, No.2, Vol.I, Chap.VII.Pp.97.

Arndt, C.O., et al. Education in China Today. Leaflet No.69, U.S. Office of Education, 1944. Pp.12.

Balme, Harold. China and Modern Medicine. London: United Council for Missionary Education, 1921. Pp.224.

Becker, Carl H., et al. The Reorganization of Education in China. Paris: League of Nations' Institute of Intellectual Cooperation, 1933. Pp.ii-200.

Bonnard, Abel. In China. New York: E. P. Dutton & Co., 1927. Pp.ix-361.

Chambers, Menitt M. Universities of the World Outside U.S.A. Washington, D.C.: American Council on Education, 1950. Pp.xvii-924.

Chang, Peng-chun. Education for Modernization in China. New York: Teachers College, Columbia University, 1923. Pp.iii-92.

Chen, Li-fu. Chinese Education During the War (1937-42). Chungking, China: Ministry of Education, 1943. Pp.ii-41

Chiang, Monlin. A Study in Chinese Principles of Education. Shanghai, China: The Commercial Press, Ltd., 1918. Pp.iii-187.

Chiang, Wen-han. The Chinese Student Movement. New York: King's Crown Press, 1948. Pp.x-176.

Chu, Yu-kuang. Some Problems of A National System of Education in China. Shanghai, China: The Commercial Press, Ltd., 1933. Pp.xiii-394.

Chuang, Chai-hsuan. Tendencies Toward A Democratic System of Education. Shanghai, China: The Commercial Press, Ltd., 1922. Pp.xvi-176.

Chung, Lu-chai. A History of Democratic Education in Modern China. Shanghai, China: The Commercial Press, Ltd., 1934. Pp.xxxiii-258.

Cressy, Earl H. Christian Higher Education in China. Shanghai, China: Christian Education Association, 1928. Pp.xii-306.

Dewey, John and Alice Chipman Dewey. Letters From China And Japan. New York: E. P. Dutton & Co., 1920. Pp.311.

Duggan, Stephen. A Critique of the Report of the League of Nations' Mission of Education Experts to China. New York: Institute of International Education, 1933. Pp.38.

Dudley, Lavinia P. "China," Encyclopedia America. New York: The American Corporation, 1953. Vol.6, 516-60.

Edmunds, Charles K. Modern Education in China. Washington, D.C.: Government Printing Office, 1919. Pp.72.

Ford, Eddy L. The History of the Educational Work of the Methodist Episcopal Church in China. New York: Christian Herald Mission Press, 1938. Pp.294.

Forster, Lancelot. The New Culture in China. London: G. Allen & Unwin, Ltd., 1936. Pp.ii-240.

————. English Ideals in Education For Chinese Students. Shanghai, China: The Commercial Press, Ltd., 1936. Pp.vi-177.

Freyer, John. The Educational Reform in China. U.S.Office of Education, Report 1909, Vol.1, 513-21.

Freyn, Hubert. Chinese Education in the War. Shanghai, China: Kelly & Walsh Co., 1940. Pp.iv-137.

Galt, Howard S. A History of Chinese Educational Institutions. London: Arthur Prosthain, 1951. Pp. ix-394.

Graybill, Henry B. The Educational Reform in China. Hongkong; 1911. Pp.iii-138.

Ho, Yen-sun. Chinese Education From the Western Viewpoint. Abstract of Ph.D. dissertation, Chicago University, Chicago, 1913. Pp.vi-91.

Hsiao, En-cheng. The History of Chinese Education in China. Peking, China: Peking University Press, 1932. Pp.xiv-164.

Hubbard, George D. Education in Chengtu, Szechwan. New York: The Pedogogical Seminary, 1922. Vol.29, No.3.

Hutchinson, Paul. China's Real Revolution. New York: Missionary Education Movement of the United States and Canada, 1924. Pp.x-182.

Hwee, Lee Teng. The Problem of New Education in China. Bruges, Belgium: A Moens-Patfoort, 1911. Pp.12.

Keyte, John. In China Now. London: United Council for Missionary Education, 1923. Pp.160.

King, H. E. The Educational System of China. Washington, D.C.: Government Printing Office, 1911. Pp. 105.

Kuo, Ping-wen. The Chinese System of Public Education. New York: Teachers College, Columbia University, 1915. Pp.xii-209.

Latourette, Kenneth S. The Chinese; Their History And Culture. New York: The Macmillan Co., 1934. 2 vols.

————. The Development of China. Boston: Houghton Mifflin Co., 1920. Pp.xii-309.

—————. History of Christian Missions in China. New York: The Macmillan Co., 1929. Pp.xii-930.

—————. China Under the Republic. New York: Institute of International Education, 1921. Pp.23.

Lew, Timothy T. The Contribution of Christian Colleges and Universities to the Church in China. Shanghai, China: Educational Association, 1924. Pp.13.

Martin, W.A.P. The Chinese: Their Education, Philosophy and Letters. New York: Harper and Bros., 1881. Pp.iv-319

—————. Hanlin Papers. London: Trubner & Co., 1880. Pp.vi-393.

McCormick, Patrick J. and Francis P. Cassidy. History of Education. Washington, D.C.: The Catholic Education Press, 1953. Pp.xxvi-688.

Monroe, Paul. China: A Nation in Evolution. New York: The Macmillan Co., 1928. Pp.xv-447.

MacNair, Harley F. Voices From Unoccupied China. Chicago: Chicago University Press, 1944. Pp.iv-106.

Purcell, Victor W. Problems of Chinese Education. London: Paul, Trench, Trubner & Co., 1936. Pp.viii-261.

Rowbotham, Arnold H. Missionary and Mandarin. University of California Press, 1942. Pp.xi-374.

Russell, Bertrand R. The Problem of China. London: G Allen and Unwin, Ltd., 1922. Pp.ii-260.

Ryan, Thomas F. China Through Catholic Eyes. Hongkong: Catholic Truth Society,1941. Pp.v-149.

Soothill, William E. China and Education; with special reference to the university for China. London: Central Asian Society, 1912. Pp.16.

Stephen, King-Hall. Western Civilization and the Far East. London: Methuen & Co., 1930. Pp.365.

Sze, Sao-ki Alfred. Reconstruction in China; address of His Excellency, the Chinese Minister, Sao-ki Alfred Sze, at the meeting of American Academy of Political and Social Science, Philadelphia, Nov. 27th, 1934. New York: The Chinese Culture Society, 1934. Pp.15.

Tao, W.T. and C.P. Chen. Education in China. Shanghai, China: The Commercial Press, Ltd., 1925. Pp.iii-39.

Teng, Tsui-yang. Education in China. Peking, China: The Society for the Study of International Education, 1923. Pp.227.

Twiss, George R. Science and Education in China. Shanghai, China: The Commercial Press, Ltd., 1925. Pp.ix-361.

United Boards for Christian Colleges in China. The Story of the Christian Colleges of China. New York: United Boards for Christian Colleges in China, 1935. Pp.16.

Van Dorn, Harold A. Twenty Years of the Chinese Republic. New York: A. A. Knopf, 1932. Pp.xiv-309.

Vinacke, Harold M. A History of the Far East in Modern Times. New York: Appleton Century Crofts, Inc., 1950. Pp.xix-785.

Wang, Shih-chieh. Education in China. Shanghai, China: China United Press, 1935. Pp.45.

Webster, J.B. Christian Education and the National Consciousness in China. New York: E. P. Dutton & Co., 1923. Pp.xi-323.

————. The Spirit of Chinese Culture. New York: C. Scribner's Sons, 1947. Pp.xii-186.

Yin, Chi-ling. Reconstruction of Modern Educational Organization in China. Shanghai, China: The Commercial Press, Ltd., 1924. Pp.xiii-171.

Yu, Ping Paul. Eyes East. Paterson, New Jersey: St. Anthony Guild Press, 1945. Pp.ix-181.

Unpublished Materials

Anderson, Mary R. "Protestant Schools for Girls in South China." Unpublished Ph.D. dissertation, Teachers College, Columbia University, New York, 1943. Pp.xxvii-365.

Chen, Ching-szu. "The Significance for Religious Education of Modern Educational Trends in China." Unpublished Ph.D. dissertation, University of Iowa, 1940. Pp.xii-231.

Chu, Yu-kuang. "Some Problems of A National System of Education in China in the Light of Comparative Education." Unpublished Ph.D. dissertation, Teachers College, Columbia University, New York, 1930. Pp.viii-390.

Gregg, Alice H. "China and Educational Autonomy; the Changing Role of the Protestant Education Missionary in China." Unpublished Ph.D. dissertation, Syracuse University, New York, 1946. Pp.xvi-285.

Peake, Cyrus H. "Nationalism and Education in Modern China." Unpublished Ph.D. dissertation, Teachers College, Columbia University, New York, 1932. Pp.xiv-240.

Rugh, A. D. "American Influence in China's Changing Education." Unpublished Ph.D. dissertation, University of Washington, Seattle, 1940. Pp.iv-207.

Tsang, Chiu-sam. "Nationalism in School Education in China Since the Opening of the Twentieth Century." Unpublished Ph.D. dissertation, Teachers College, Columbia University, New York, 1933. Pp.vii-241.

Newspapers and Periodicals

Bulletin of the China Christian Educational Association, 1924-33. Shanghai, China.

Bulletin of China Institute in America, June, 1926, New York City.

Bulletin of the Chinese National Association for the Advancement of Education, vol. II, Nos.4-8, 1923. Peiping, China.

China Christian Educational Quarterly, March, 1940. Shanghai, China.

China Educational Review, 1929-1932. Shanghai, China.

Chinese Recorder, December, 1940. Shanghai, China.

Les Missions Catholiques de Chine, 1938. Shanghai, China.

Newsweek, December 1, 1944; April 15, 1946. New York City.

Rock Magazine, April, 1937. Shanghai, China.

South China Morning Post, November 14, 1928. Hongkong.

Times Educational Supplement, July 21, 1945. New York City.

Periodical Articles

"American Colleges in China," School and Society, XXV (April, 1927), 422-23.

"Annual Report of the Catholic University of Peiping, 1939-40," Digest of the Synodal Commission, XIII (December, 1940), 990-98.

"Annual Report of the Catholic University of Peiping, 1938-39," Digest of the Synodal Commission, XII (September, 1939), 891-97.

"Aurora University of Shanghai Opens Magnificant New Building," Far Eastern Review, XXXII (September, 1936), 389-97.

Balme, Harold. "Facts Concerning the School of Medicine of Shangtung Christian University," Educational Review, XII (July, 1920), 223-26.

Bisson, T. B. "Formal Opening of Yenching University," China Weekly Review, L (September, 1929), 84-86.

Caldwell, O. J. "Christian Colleges in New China," Far Eastern Survey, XI (November16, 1942), 236-37.

Carrol, Thomas. "The Educational Work of the Catholic Missions in China," Digest of the Synodal Commission, XIV (January, 1941), 39-54.

Castleton, A. G. "University Education in Wartime China," Journal of Education, London, LXXIII (December, 1941), 537-41.

"Catholic University of Peking," Catholic World, CXXIX (June, 1929), 343-45.

————————————, Digest of the Synodal Commission, II (May, 1929), 341-50.

————————————, Digest of the Synodal Commission, X (January, 1937), 66-71.

————————————, The Shield, IV (January, 1940), 12-15.

Chen, Chi-pao. "Twenty-five Years of Modern Education in China," The Chinese Social and Political Science Review, XII (July, 1928), 452-54.

Chen, Li-fu. "Chinese Universities During the War," Educational Record, XXIV (April, 1943), 130-35.

Chen, Y. G. "Brief Survey of the Contribution of the University of Nanking to the Life of the Community," Educational Review China, XXV (January, 1933), 62-64.

Chiang, Monlin. "Higher Education in China," The Educational Journal, IX (November, 1936), 10-12.

"China's Christian Anchor," Literary Digest, LXXXII (September, 1924), 34-37.

"China Salvages Its College Students," School and Society, LI (June, 1940), 701.

"China's Universities Expanded Despite the War," School and Society, LVI (October, 1942), 321-22.

"Chinese Higher Education," China Institute Bulletin, IV (October, 1939), 2-8.

Chu, Y. "Effects of the Present Sino-Japanese War on Higher Education in China," School and Society, XLVII (April, 1938), 443-46.

Cline, John W. "Soochow University," The Educational Review, XI (January, 1919), 75-77.

"Communist Authorities Have Taken Over the Catholic University of Fu Jen," Tablet, CXCVI (October, 1950), 354-56.

"The Constitution of the Tientsin University," Digest of the Synodal Commission, II (February, 1929), 82-89.

Crawford, D. L. "Universities in China," Educational Review China, XXV (April, 1932), 128-31.

Cressey, George B. "Educational Problems in China," American Association of University Professors Bulletin, XXXI (Spring, 1945), 18-27.

Cressy, Earl H. "Correlated Program for Christian Higher Education in China," International Review of Missions, XXII (April, 1933), 240-50.

__________. "Council of Higher Education," Educational Review China, XXVI (April, 1934), 203-12.

__________. "Council of Higher Education, Annual Meeting, Shanghai, January, 1936," Educational Review China, XXVIII (March, 1936), 113-19.

Decker, J. W. "Christian Higher Education in China," Far Eastern Survey, XV (April, 1946), 124-26.

Dennett, Tyler. "The Missionary Schoolmaster," Asia, XVII (March, 1918), 211-22.

"Descration of Shanghai College By Japanese Army," China Weekly Review, LXXXV (June, 1938), 41-42.

Donovan, John F. "Schools Count in China," American Ecclesiastical Review, CXXV (November, 1951), 378-80.

Edmunds, Charles K. "Modern Education in China," Bureau of Education Bulletin, XLIV (1919), 50-54.

"Education in Communist China," World Today, VIII (June, 1950), 257-68.

"Educational Union in Central China," The Missionary Review of the World, LIV (August, 1931), 628-29.

Espino, Rafael B. "Impressions From A Recent Trip to China," Philippiné Agriculturist, XXIV (Jan., 1936), 619-21.

Fitch, Robert F. "Hangchow Christian College," The Missionary Review of the World, XLVII (March, 1924), 228-30.

Fitzgerald, Thomas R. "Missioners in Secular Universities," China Missionary Bulletin, I (March, 1949), 225-26.
Forster, L. "Higher Education in China," Contemporary Review, CLXX (April, 1946), 88-93.
Han, Lih-wu. "University of Nanking Enters Its Fifth Decade," China Weekly Review, XLIX (June, 1929), 81-85.
Hanson, H.E. "Stalking the Educational Bugbear in Peiping," China Weekly Review, LXXIV (November, 1935), 386-87.
Heimichs, Maurus. "De Loco et Munere Jesu Christi en Universo," Digest of the Synodal Commission, XII (December, 1939), 1135-1148.
Herman, C. E. "Higher Education in China," School and Society, XLII (November, 1935), 676-77.
"History of Aurora University," Digest of the Synodal Commission, I (November, 1928), 413-19.
Hubbard, George D. "Education in Chengtu, Szechwan," Educational Review, XIV (January, 1922), 23-24.
"Jesuit Mission Vignettes," Jesuit Missions, IV (October, 1930), 211-12.
Jonghe, de George. "Catholic Education in China," Jesuit Missions, V (April, 1931), 96-98.
Kao, John B. "National Catholic Educational Congress, Feb.15-21, 1948," China Missionary Bulletin, II (1948), 133-53.
Koo, T. Z. "Chinese Education Under War Conditions," School and Society, LI (June, 1940), 701.
Lacy, C. G. "China's Immigrant Colleges and Middle Schools," China Weekly Review, XCIV (September 21, 1940), 84-85.
Lewis, Robert E. "The Empress Dowager's System of Modern Colleges for China," Review of Reviews, XXVI (July, 1902), 72-74.
Lin, C. Y. "Yenching University Establishes Ceramic Research Laboratory," American Ceramic Society Bulletin, XIV (April, 1935), 148-50.
Lloyd, Ralph W. "Christian Colleges and Middle Schools in China," Association American Colleges Bulletin, XXXV (October, 1949), 437-40.
Lo, R. E. "Education in the Chinese Hills," Atlantic Monthly, CLXXIII (January, 1944), 92-96.
Mao, Kun. "The Tenth Anniversary of the Boone Library School," Boone Library School Quarterly, II (June, 1930), 137-38.

Meng, P. C. "Japan's War on Chinese Higher Education," Foreign Affairs, XVI (January, 1938), 351-54.
Nash, V. "Threaten to Close Mission Colleges," Christian Century, XLVIII (April, 1931), 488-89.
"New Hostel For University," Digest of the Synodal Commission, II (January, 1929), 22-28.
Park, N. Y. "Educators of New China Speak," School and Society, XXXVIII (November 18, 1933), 678-80.
Paton, D. M. "Christian Work in Chinese Government Universities," International Review of Missions, XXXIII (April, 1944), 152-62.
Patton, C. E. "University of Nanking Controls China's Famine Relief Fund," China Weekly Review, LXVII (December, 1933), 68-70.
Pott, P. L. Hawks. "Christian Education in China," China Quarterly, I (March, 1936), 47-53.
Powell, J. B. "Soochow University Elects Chinese President," China Weekly Review, LXII (September, 1927), 106-107.
Radcliffe-Brown A. R. "Chinese Centers of Learning," School and Society, XLIX (March 18, 1939), 350-52.
Read, B. E. "The Peking Union Medical College," The Missionary Review of the World, XLIV (December, 1921), 925-28.
"The Report of the Council of Higher Education of Christian Colleges Association in China, 1947," Lingnan University Bulletin, I (1948), 109-112.
Rouleau, Francis A. "Chen Tan: A Chinese Catholic University," America, L (December, 1933), 295-97.
Seng, Samuel T. "Miss Mary Elizabeth Wood, the Queen of the Modern Library Movement in China," Boone Library School Quarterly, III (September,1931), 9-11.
Serviere, Joseph de La. "The Work of the Catholic Church in China," The Chinese Recorder, XLIV (Oct., 1913), 625-28.
"Shanghai College Now A University," Missionary Review of the World, LIV (October, 1931), 786-88.
"Some New Educational Developments in China," China Weekly Review, CXIV (September, 1949), 37-41.
Standard, Henry K. "Private Educational Institutions," China Missionary Bulletin, II (August, 1950), 661-62.
Stuart, J. Leighton. "Formal Opening of Yenching University, Peiping," Missionary Review of the World, LIII (February, 1930), 98-99.

———————. "Crisis in Christian Higher Education in China," China Weekly Review, XLVI (November, 1928), 319-20.

Tao, Frank C. H. "War and China's Colleges," China Weekly Review, LXXXVI (October, 1938), 226-27.

Tang, P. "Chinese Universities on the March," American Scholar, X (January, 1941), 41-48.

"Three Years of People's Education," Chinese Youth Bulletin, III (October, 1952), 5-6.

Thruston, Lawrence. "Ginling College," Educational Review, X (July, 1918), 242-43.

"Universities in Tientsin," China Missionary Bulletin, II (April, 1950), 403-404.

"University Graduates' Letter to Mao Tse-tung," China Missionary Bulletin, II (October, 1950), 853-54.

"University Reforms Prescribed by Ministry of Education," China Weekly Review, LXIX (April, 1934), 416-17.

Willier, Richard. "Catholic Church in Shanghai," China Missionary Bulletin, IV (December, 1932), 797-798.

Wittfogel, K. A. "Culture Is War; Is the Bombing of Chinese Universities Caprice or Policy?" Asia, XXXVIII (April, 1938), 216-19.

Wu, Hung-sze. "The Past, Present, and Future of Boone Library School," Boone Library School Quarterly, I (January, 1929), 108-116.

"The Yale-in-China Twenty-fifth Anniversary," School and Society, XXXIV (November, 1936), 427-28.

"Yale-in-China Observes 30th Anniversary in Changsha," China Weekly Review, LXXVIII (November, 1936), 427-28.

Yang, Yung-ching. "Education in Wartime China," Association of American Colleges Bulletin, XXIX (March, 1943), 60-69.

Young, C. F. "Higher Education in China," Peabody Journal of Education, XIV (January, 1937), 185-95.

Yu, J. S. "Education in Communist China," China Missionary Bulletin, III (September, 1950), 742-48.

Yu, Wu. "Kunming College Life," China Weekly Review, LXXXIX (April, 1939), 397-98.